Lead With Your Heart

Sell Happiness
and You and Your Business
Will Flourish

Lewis Green

HRD Press, Inc. • **Amherst** • **Massachusetts**

Published by: HRD Press, Inc.
22 Amherst Road
Amherst, MA 01002
1-800-822-2801 (U.S. and Canada)
413-253-3488
413-253-3490 (FAX)
www.hrdpress.com

ISBN: 978-1-59996-120-0

Cover design by Eileen Klockars
Editorial services by Suzanne Bay
Production services by Anctil Virtual Office

Table of Contents

Acknowledgments

No one writes a book without lots of help from others. Therefore, the right thing to do is to give those who contributed to this book a great round of thanks.

In no particular order, I want to thank all those whose ideas, thoughts, writings, and passions contributed to the contents, especially Starbucks's Howard Schultz for whom I once worked, and author-researcher Jim Collins, whose writings and workshops taught me much. Ken Lizotte, my agent and "thought leader" who guided me every step of the way and who stepped in to help me through the hills and valleys that rise and dip during any project this large. Kate Victory, whose editing and comments helped shape and polish my work. A special thanks to everyone at HRD Press, without whom this book would not have seen the light of day. I especially want to thank my editor, Suzanne Bay, whose suggestions, prodding, and thoughtful explanations and recommendations saved the reader from plodding through some difficult passages, and Robert W. Carkhuff, publisher, for his confidence in *Lead With Your Heart*. Last here but first in my life, my wife Kay, who has stood by me for 33 years, and always encouraged my writing.

Introduction

We must be the change we wish to see in the world.

— Mahatma Gandhi

Lead With Your Heart introduces a business model that will result in business success as measured by business growth, revenues, and profits, as well as create a better world in which to do business, to work, and to live. Of course, for any model to work, you must believe, you must be passionate in that belief, and you must work hard to achieve your business goals and objectives.

This book is about changing the way we do business. It is written to inspire executives, managers, and entrepreneurs to invest in a new business model that can be a first step to changing the world we live in.

Why do I write such a book? I look around and see a beautiful planet with beautiful people, where all things seem possible and there is no shortage of enthusiasm and brilliance. Nevertheless, our forests and waters are diminishing, wars flourish, and greed prompts malfeasance within our business ranks. We are living in dangerous times.

Is it getting worse, or is it the worst of times? I don't know — that sort of thinking is relative and not helpful. We need to go forward, and use what we learn from the past to improve our future — not dwell on history in ways that keep us from having a positive vision.

But what I do know is that governments are ineffective when it comes to creating positive and long-lasting change. Businesses, on the other hand, prepare for change and usually embrace it because they expect it and realize that they must be prepared for it. They have in place the best practices and innovative thinking to use change as a means to improve themselves. Business and work in general is where we spend at least a third of our lives. Businesses, then, present the perfect launching pad from which to make the world a better place, while at the same time producing great products and services as well as enough profit to pay fair wages and provide needed benefits.

This book is about such change. It is about creating an environment where business leaders lead with the heart: They do it by taking a hard look at their values, implementing and living by those values, and then building value-driven enterprises in which people are more important than overzealousness to earn money. In this book, we talk about creating happiness because by doing this, we change the world in good and right ways.

Defining happiness is not an easy task. This book is dedicated to painting a picture of what happiness looks like from a business perspective. Briefly, when I define *happiness,* I am talking about meeting and exceeding people's wants, needs, and desires by creating great experiences for employees, customers, and citizens that our businesses touch. I am talking about putting the "who" (people) first, not the "what" (profits). By doing so, we create happiness, contribute to better living, and create and deliver products and services that people want and need at prices that deliver value.

I often wonder why American businesses don't spend more time strategizing around happiness. It is true that many companies are customer-focused and thus invest lots of energy in meeting customer needs. Responding to those needs should result in happy customers, happy employees, and a healthy bottom line. Unfortunately, the efforts being made by too many businesses to create happy and loyal customers fall far short of what is necessary. We explore why that is throughout this book.

Who Should Read This Book?

If you are an entrepreneur, business owner, executive, director, manager, or wannabe leader and you suspect that leading with your heart, working with passion, and caring about the bottom line are good for you, good for your shareholders, good for your employees, and good for your customers, this book is for you.

Be warned, however: I may shake you up some, and I will propose strategies, ideas, and recommendations that require total commitment from you and everyone in your business, so you can reap the rewards of your maximum potential. The research and the ideas come from some of the best business people in America. I learned and borrowed and put them into practice myself, and share them now out of a passion for the wisdom they represent.

In summary, this book is about remaining true to your values, always meeting customers' needs, and getting and staying completely focused on happiness.

Chapter One
Measuring Business Success

Happiness matters.

Happiness is the driving force behind everything Americans do. It is the key to determining their wants, needs, and desires. It is the essence of the American Dream, and it is as important as the air you breathe. Even our Declaration of Independence calls for the pursuit of happiness. And yet a 2006 study by the Pew Research Center found that only 34 percent of Americans consider themselves "very happy" and 50 percent consider themselves "pretty happy." Fifteen percent report that they are "not too happy."

One of the most popular courses at Harvard University is about happiness and creating "a fulfilling and flourishing life." In fact, the course "Positive Psychology" outdraws "Introductory Economics." That scares me. Have we gone so far down the road of work, power, and greed that we need to be taught about happiness?

I believe these examples point to an overactive, over-achieving, over-stressed population chasing after broken dreams. On the other hand, this information points to an untapped market your business can penetrate. The savvy business person will do everything possible to ensure that his or her business is people-centered and not primarily focused on the bottom line. My belief is that if *you* do good, your business will do well.

Don't jump to conclusions, however. I do not advise firing your CFO, your accountant, or your financial adviser. My argument does not pit happiness against financial responsibility and healthy margins. Instead, I argue for strong fiscal responsibility and budgets that create better-than-hoped-for margins, by focusing on happiness to grow success and the bottom line (but never falsely). Everything you do must be authentic to a culture built on values. Business leaders are responsible for creating happiness within the organization and responsible for the bottom line.

From the various reports I've read, it seems that at least 65 percent of all Americans want great business experiences that will help make them happy. Even the "very happy" folks can be moved to a higher happiness level, creating even greater customer-conversion opportunities for business.

Research tells us that happy people are more productive and live longer lives. One study of a Catholic religious community concluded that nuns who had a positive outlook in their 20s live as much as 10 years longer than those who are less positive. Another research project focused on a group of people who each kept a daily diary for six months, recording only those things that went well on any given day. The conclusion was that these participants were happier and healthier than those participants who did not focus on positive thinking. Both studies imply that businesses could increase productivity and attendance by focusing on happiness in the workplace.

The conclusions of these and other studies act as the foundation of this book's business philosophy: Happiness has more to do with our state of mind than with the state of our bank account.

Lead With Your Heart offers a philosophy that great businesses — large and small — will create better places to work, contribute positively to their communities and to the environment, and produce products and services that result in happy customers and clients IF they embrace the law of reciprocity (giving is getting) and are people-focused, not money-focused.

In *Lead With Your Heart,* I do not suggest that happiness waits just around the corner and it is easily within our grasp. Happiness defined in the *Lead With Your Heart* business model looks like this:

1. The organization is people-centered. People come before profit in every instance.

2. The organization's values center on making the world a better place to live and work.

3. The organization understands the wants, needs, and desires of its employees and its customers.

4. It creates products, services, value, prices, and most important, experiences that meet or exceed people's wants, needs, and desires.

Only a blind, dumb, and extremely arrogant business community would ignore the data and the business potential inherent in making people happier — and not just consumers. In fact, perhaps stronger: the company's employees have to feel a sense of happiness about the company they work for and the work they do if the company's customers and clients are to experience levels of happiness that keep them coming back.

Every week, you and I have "negative" consumer experiences. Apparently the world is full of business managers unable to imagine and create customer experiences that make us happier or that are built upon solid, trustworthy, credible, and uplifting values. Profit shouldn't be the primary force behind success.

Citizens Financial Group is one business that strives diligently to create an experience that fulfills my image of happiness. Banks don't normally do a great job providing positive and memorable experiences, but this bank gets it. Its Web site gives you a hint of why people are the center of their business:

"In 1828, Citizens Financial Group got its start as a small community bank called the High Street Bank in Providence, Rhode Island. In 1871, the directors of High Street Bank established Citizens Savings Bank. Its first deposit was from Miss Jessie Grant, the daughter of the bank's vice president. The firm has since grown to have $155 billion in assets, making it the 8th largest commercial bank holding company in the United States. Owned by The Royal Bank of Scotland Group, the company has branches in 13 states and non-branch offices in more than 30 states. But while we've grown in size, we still try to provide every customer with the same friendly, personal service Miss Jessie Grant received that very first day."

The company's *Citizens Credo* (distributed only internally) asks that each employee live their work lives in the following way:

Customers

Treat the customer the way you would love to be treated all the time.

Colleagues

Do what it takes to make Citizens the best place to work in the world.

Community

Show that you care deeply about the community. Conduct yourself ethically all the time.

It is not unusual for a business to have a credo or guiding principles. However, it is all too frequently the case that businesses do not live up to what they claim to stand for. Citizens Financial employees do a very good job of living up to their credo in their interactions with people.

Ultimately, your fate as a business person, be it entre-preneur, executive, owner, middle manager, or lower-level employee, comes down to the "who" — not the "what." So it only makes sense to spend most of your time thinking about what makes people happy and what doesn't.

The pursuit of happiness does not rest on some shaky psychological definition of being happy. Throughout this book, I lay out what it takes to create customer and employee experiences that develop customer loyalty, create a great brand image, increase sales, and grow the bottom line. In essence, I am talking about building businesses that revolve around customers and employees, that are built on values, and that deliver experiences that exceed expectations. That is what I call happiness.

The Story Begins

On a big lake in the Pacific Northwest sits a large and elegant estate, complete with swimming pool, an orchard, forested landscapes, a spacious main house and several smaller houses, a boat dock, and grand views of the lake and city beyond.

The Sisters of St. Joseph of Peace live here. In addition to practicing their mission of peace through justice, they possess the business skills of America's greatest CEOs. Some of them are entrepreneurs, and some are executives. Their neighbors include Bill Gates.

Across the lake sits another birthplace of success— Starbucks. While salaries are relatively modest, potential wealth in the form of stock options and excellent benefits is available to all who work a specified minimum of hours, supplemented bountifully with something difficult to measure: happiness, based on generosity and values. The first place is the home of a religious order, the second the headquarters of a business giant. The differences might seem obvious: The nuns in the religious community don't choose making money as their goal, and they live modestly despite their surroundings. On the other hand, Starbucks works diligently to make a profit.

What could these two groups possibly have in common? It's simple: Both organizations strive to create happiness for themselves and those they touch and approach their respective missions with love, passion, commitment, and dedication. Neither group measures success solely by the amount of money they possess or the images they project. Both organizations lead with their hearts.

That is the lesson I want to explore in this book. Business and personal success can be measured in terms of revenue, which may or may not deliver happiness to the wealth makers, the workers, or the customers. I believe there is a better way to measure business. The nuns and Starbucks leaders demonstrate that way.

Religious orders reach out to lift people up in any number of ways—by educating, offering health care, providing shelter to the homeless, and feeding the poor. In these ways they contribute to the well-being of those they serve.

Now move from the spiritual to the mundane: Walk into a Starbucks store and watch employees interacting with the customers. You will see happiness. It comes from what Starbucks calls the "third place experience."

Enter the headquarters building and you will see more of the same, as well as the stress and the angst that comes from working in any business. Since its founding, Starbucks has made billions of dollars. Starbucks, however, does not exist solely to make money and does not measure its success only in that way. In fact, Starbucks does not exist only to sell coffee: Its lifeblood is creating an experience that results in happiness, even though the company doesn't use that word to describe it.

How does Starbucks measure success? Here is its Mission Statement and the set of guiding principles:

Starbucks Mission Statement

*Establish Starbucks as the premier purveyor of the finest coffee in the world **while maintaining our uncompromising principles while we grow.***

Guiding Principles

The following six guiding principles will help us measure the appropriateness of our decisions:

1. Provide a great work environment and treat each other with respect and dignity.

2. Embrace diversity as an essential component in the way we do business.

3. Apply the highest standards of excellence to the purchasing, roasting and fresh delivery of our coffee.

4. Develop enthusiastically satisfied customers all of the time.

5. Contribute positively to our communities and our environment.

6. Recognize that profitability is essential to our future success.

The first five principles have to do with leading from the heart and mind (and, as a result, creating happiness).

Happiness touches everyone.

This is a good time to take a breath and further define happiness for you. Some people think of happiness as a kind of satisfaction. I argue that it extends miles beyond satisfaction. It does not often have to do with laughter or fun, although fun sometimes is part of it. Instead, the happiness I talk about within these pages comes from the center of our being, close to our hearts and deep within our psyches. You know it when you experience it, and so do your customers.

Starbucks is not the only example of what this business paradigm looks like. I could have used a number of small, mid-sized, and large companies as examples of a holistic approach to business, where profits are essential to success yet are only one factor used to measure success. You can read about many of them in *Built to Last* by James C. Collins and Jerry I. Porras.

These companies make it because they give back to their leaders, their workers, their stockholders, their customers, their communities, and their environments. Their business models are based on ethics, morals, and more often than not, happiness.

Do they represent some likeness to Nirvana? Of course not. They are led by humans who sometimes make mistakes. The lesson, however, is that such companies make better places to work, contribute positively to their communities and to the environment, and produce products and services that result in happy customers and clients.

The differences between a company that is led with the heart and a company that is led by the bottom line are pretty clear, as you can see:

Happiness Model	Results	Bottom-Line Model	Results
To build a business culture internally, based on happiness	• Increased productivity • Decreased employee turnover • Customer-focused employees	To build a business culture internally, based on the bottom line	• Average industry productivity • Increased employee turnover • Internally focused employees
To create great customer experiences that exceed expectations	• Increased sales • Loyal customers • Customers who encourage others to purchase from your business	To create good products and services that meet or exceed customer expectations	• Average industry sales • Customers looking for a deal • A business like any other that fails to generate customer referrals

(continued)

(continued)

Happiness Model	Results	Bottom-Line Model	Results
To focus on the "who" (people), not the "what" (things businesses do)	• Employees concerned with creating products and services that meet or exceed customers' wants, needs, and desires • Customer service that is the best in your industry	To focus on the "what" (things businesses do) and not the "who" (people)	• Good products and services that might meet customers' wants, needs, and desires • Average and uneven customer service
To market and sell experiences	Focus is on: • Creating great customer experiences that exceed customer expectations • Creating loyal customers who buy value, not price • Increasing margins	To market and sell products and services	Focus is on: • Making and selling products and services that may meet customer expectations but are seldom better or worse than competitors' products and services • Getting customers to shop for price, not value • Decreasing margins

(continued)

(concluded)

Happiness Model	Results	Bottom-Line Model	Results
To live by our values	Values are about people (not products and services). Everything you say and do is measured against each value. If something violates any value's standards, it is not said or done.	To live by the bottom line	Values are frequently ignored, leading to a lowering of credibility and trust within the minds and hearts of employees and customers (and, in some instances, costly lawsuits)
To hire people who believe in your business's values and to fire those who don't	Builds a culture that is people-centered and happy, where workers want to exceed expectations, and be innovative and creative	To hire people with skills and are willing to work hard	Builds a culture that is not people-centered, resulting in a "that's not my job" work ethic and a "this is how we do it here" attitude, diminishing the value of innovation and creativity

This Happiness business model for success also results in profits and wealth. Sometimes the wealth is measured in big, fat, tall stacks of green but sometimes it is measured by smaller stacks. It is always measured by a happy heart.

Business people come in all shapes and sizes, all degrees of intellects and personalities, and all varieties of experiences. Not everyone accepts the philosophy I'm talking about or these ways of doing business. In fact, some will scoff at it—and that, I believe, is their loss.

Happiness, Commitment, and Hard Work

Some of you have probably flashed back to the '60s and suspect that I swallowed too many pills or smoked too much of the sweet-smelling herb. Let me assure you that I have no illusions about the intelligence, stiff spine, and sweat equity it takes to create a successful business. I will discuss those things necessary to create success in subsequent chapters of this book.

So, if you are prepared to put in the time and sweat (and money, if you own your business) to make your business succeed and add a little heart to it, let's get on with it.

And remember: Hard work, structure, planning, and fiscal responsibility can be combined with happiness and wealth for all, without sacrificing the bottom line.

Failure

If you listen to the claims of some so-called experts about business failures, you might conclude that business people stand at the precipice of failure. Not so. Most businesses fail because the owners filed individual bankruptcy.

Great! Most entrepreneurs, business owners, and business managers succeed. Does that mean the odds of succeeding and making tons of money are weighted heavily in your favor? Not so fast! Statistics recorded by the Administrative Office of the U.S. Courts fail to reflect mediocrity and the guilt and anguish people feel when they have to work for leaders who bring pain into their employees' lives and into their customers' lives.

This book is not about being average, nor is it supportive of mediocrity or exploitation or pain. It is about being the best you and your business can be.

Like business people, business failures and mediocrity come in many shapes and sizes. Time and time again I hear business people proclaim that they just want to break even and maybe make a little money. They set easy goals and don't stretch themselves because they fear failure (or success). Many bow to the boardrooms of America that demand only short-term results.

Maximizing business potential does not come easily or at all for these business leaders, because becoming the best you can be is not about playing it safe and just trying to make today's buck. It is about long-term results and calculated risk-taking, and it will require lots of stretching.

Howard Schultz, the visionary guru behind Starbucks, lived on no income for several years after raising the capital to purchase the company from its original owners. His sacrifice paid off big-time for Howard and his employees. Their hard work also paid off for the millions of coffee drinkers who thrive on the Starbucks experience: the baristas know your name, serve your needs, and meet your wants. The *"third place experience"* provides a place where you can go to get away. Pleasure and satisfaction are planned down to every single detail, and the company strives to build customer and partner satisfaction into everything it does. It serves as one example of the many organizations that understand people and how to make them happy. Sometimes these businesses fail to meet people's wants and needs. They are not perfect. However, they always try to exceed our expectations and create happiness that spreads across cultures, classes, and personal preferences.

Do you have the guts, know-how, vision, time, and financial wherewithal to create success, to lead with the heart, and to achieve a clear but far-away vision? Harley-Davidson, 3M, HP, and GE do. Each one is a super brand, and each is focused on making tons of money, while selling varying degrees and various kinds of happiness. Not a single one is perfect, nor do they operate on identical business models. But each understands the importance of values, each makes every effort to lead with the heart, and each counts on happiness.

The core purpose of *Lead With Your Heart* is to present a business model that combines the best of today's business models with new and innovative thinking that leads to making the world a better place to live and do business, while positively affecting the bottom lines of businesses that implement and execute this model. This book is your guide.

The General Electric Way under CEO Jack Welch

General Electric's Mission Statement from 1981 through 1995 under CEO Jack Welch is described this way in Welch's best-selling book, *Winning*: "To be the most competitive enterprise in the world by being No. 1 or No. 2 in every market—fixing, selling, or closing every underperforming business that couldn't get there."

Being competitive is not synonymous with being the best, if you define "best" based on results as perceived by the customers, clients, and employees you serve. Welch suggests that being the best means being No. 1 or No. 2 in every market (which, in this case, relates directly to revenues).

If you work for a company with this mission, I suspect at least some of you would do anything possible to achieve the goal — perhaps things that are unethical or beyond the boundaries. Welch specifically calls for playing by the rules and expresses his personal belief in integrity, but every business person and every athlete knows about stretching the rules.

I set out in this book to show another kind of "winning" that is inclusive, rather than exclusive, and that does not shun competitiveness or make it the central theme of a mission statement. I want every business to instead strive to be the best it can be, the most innovative it can be, the most honest and trustworthy it can be, and the greatest business it can be in its industrial arena. And so I encourage you to align your missions and values in order to achieve those goals, but always with an eye to making the world better, instead of just making individuals wealthier.

I am a fan of Jim Collins and his book *Good to Great*. Collins tells us how so-called geniuses seldom build great management teams and great companies — they don't see a need to. Instead, they focus on "where to drive the bus and a road map for driving the bus." Then they enlist highly capable people to make the vision real. Great companies focus first on getting the right people together and then figuring out the best way to become great.

Collins and others make sure that everyone has a role to play. Creating a culture that is people-centered falls more into the Collins definition of *rigorous* instead of ruthless, which often is the driver behind bottom-line business models.

"To be ruthless means hacking and cutting, especially in difficult times, or wantonly firing people without any thoughtful consideration." Collins, instead, recommends that companies create rigorous cultures.

"To be rigorous means consistently applying exacting standards at all times and at all levels, especially in upper management. To be rigorous, not ruthless, means that the best people need not worry about their positions and can concentrate fully on their work." What he's saying falls within the goals of leading with your heart.

Executive compensation hurts the bottom line.

When the top earners get an 883 percent increase and the bottom tier is rewarded with a decrease over 20 years, there is something terribly wrong. It is unhealthy for our economy, because 60 percent or more is dependent upon consumer spending. Consumer spending drops when pay levels do not keep pace.

I want to share one final example of a situation where greed gets in the way of productivity, prosperity, and great experiences for all.

While I was writing this book, Sikorsky Aircraft workers went on strike over what they believed were unfair hits to their health benefits. This is an era when benefits are being reduced, and the cost of health care in the U.S. is the root cause. Sikorsky's pay package is strong, and the parent company, United Technologies Corp., is highly profitable. The workers believed that this was not the time to increase their out-of-pocket health care expenses, especially when George David, CEO of United Technologies, earned more than $50 million in 2005 and corporate profits were much lower ($15–20 million).

I have been involved in strikes and strategic planning to deal with potential strikes, and I know firsthand that it is nearly impossible for an outsider to understand what is really happening because communication coming from each side is garbled and misleading to varying degrees. However, in this instance, there was one clear message sent by the company that was hurtful to Sikorsky's case and to the future of employee productivity: Management believed that one executive is worth more than several thousand workers. *That is not true.* A pay package for any CEO that looks like $50 million when you count all the stock options is bad business. It reduces a company's credibility, and smacks of greed and injustice. Paying any one person $50 million has to hurt the bottom line—how could it not?

The Academy of Management Journal in 2003 reported that its examination of 220 studies revealed that equity ownership had no consistent effects on financial performance. Another study on executive compensation published in the Summer 2002 issue of The University of Chicago

Law Review reported that stock options meant to align managerial and stockholder interests failed. These packages simply enriched senior managers because they received most of the stock options. Our goal should be not to make anyone wealthy, but instead add a benefit that can be used for a variety of purposes. Some employees only making a modest salary use their stock options to make down payments on houses, to buys cars and motorcycles, for retirement, or for a variety of other reasons. What we need to fix is the way we compensate executives and offer stock options to those who show entrepreneurial spirit, innovation, great productivity, and an ability to contribute to our short- and long-term goals.

Businesses as a rule do not intentionally do harm, nor do executives. Harm is a natural result of the culture of winning, as defined by today's standards. This book offers a different paradigm for winning and competition: It is measured by how much good is done, while still maintaining profitable margins so it can perform more good and create better and more products and services that are people-centric.

Many companies do great things. I'm simply saying that most are too narrowly focused on earning money, instead of being focused on becoming the leaders of change and greatness for all the peoples of the world. Business leaders are best equipped and have the biggest bully pulpits; they're the ones who can make this a better world, and I want them to take on this awesome and vital responsibility. Not *after* they retire from the business world, but *while they are building great businesses.*

Be the change you wish to see in the world. Lead with passion, and strive to create happiness. We need a culture change. The best of the best — our business leaders — must use their power and positions to lead that change.

Leaders reap the benefits of the reality they create.

According to a survey released in January of 2006 by the consulting firm Salary.com, 65 percent of U.S. workers are considering a job search. These are workers already employed, so their motivation comes from deep within them. The survey also points out that bosses do not know what their employees are thinking.

Why are workers looking? Those surveyed cite "increased salary, opportunities for advancement, recognition, and excitement."

Most cite increased pay as the main reason. Respondents say that a 10 percent raise would compensate for dissatisfaction with working conditions, corporate mission, discrimination, lack of advancement, and impact on health; a 12 percent raise, they say, would make up for inadequate benefits.

Instead of a 10 percent or 12 percent pay increase, shouldn't we focus on the root causes of disaffection? Raising a worker's pay is a temporary solution based on old-school thinking that workers care more about money than about having their basic emotional and psychological needs met. Workers' happiness is not raised substantially by more pay. If it were, there would not be so much employee dissatisfaction.

With few exceptions, every job people need or want has a social, a functional, and an emotional dimension. When business leaders focus on money, they speak only to the functional side of human needs. In baseball, great teams focus on pitching, defense, and offense. Why, in business, would we focus only on one factor? We do so because we are blinded by the prospect of making money, and we measure success only by counting that money.

We should set our goals to create a great culture, to keep our promises to our customers, and to create a better world, and then measure each area for success. If we do those things, we will make more money, employ better people, create more customers, and build a better world in which to live and raise our children.

We should expect some employee disaffection. It is normal. But 65 percent reflects a problem. It is in the best interests of business to change this, and you have the power to make change, because you see and work alongside your employees at least five days a week.

How can you change your organization's culture from one of greed and self-interest to one of productivity and growth? Start by listening to your workers. Conduct surveys to ferret out root causes of unhappiness. (Remember, however, that surveys are not the be-all and end-all of employee communications.) Talk to employees and customers, because they also become disaffected from business. Listen to them and hear what they are saying.

Listen to the rumors—they often reflect more truth than not. Employees are usually unhappy because business leaders do not meet their emotional and psychological needs, as well as their financial needs. Fair pay and benefits must be a factor in success, but leaders who don't lead with the heart and who don't work diligently to make the workplace, the marketplace, and their communities better tend to produce only short-term results as measured by revenues. This is a fact that cannot be ignored: Even the best leaders, more often than not, pay more attention to the bottom line than they do to the needs of people.

This tunnel vision results in turnover, less-than-great products and services, and short-term increases in productivity, followed by downturns in productivity and performance, burnout, resentment, and frustration. It builds a wall between business and the public. In the long term, this negatively affects profits and leads to losses in the billions of dollars, creating a new downward spiral reflected in downsizing, cost-cutting, and employee backlash when the economy picks up again.

Barriers to Success

You might think you fall into a different category, one more akin to that of the tens of millions of us who have the guts, know-how, and vision, yet limited time or financial wherewithal. Don't use your limited resources as an excuse. What if the great business visionaries had feared success and set their sights on the nearest targets? Starbucks chairman Howard Schultz received several hundred no's before he raised his first dollar. And he found the time—as did those he hired—to not only think big, but walk big. All along their journey, they kept people at the center of their business goals and values. People became the foundation of their business model.

Throughout America, entrepreneurs and others in business, achieve their dreams and still find time to give back. I believe anyone can do it if they have the will and the attitude and refuse to create enterprises whose sole purpose is to make money. Lack of will and a never-say-die attitude represent the only barriers to success for those of you capable of dreaming.

And therein lies some good news: You don't need to know it all. People who believe they do become micromanagers who lower productivity, instead of leaders who inspire success.

Hire and outsource for success. Build a business culture for success. Plan for success. Execute for success. And lead with the heart for success, backed up by a great CFO or CPA who keeps an eye on the bottom line.

Got the picture?

The foundation of success is a mixture of values, ethics, and a great passion to grow the business in ways that make the world a better place. If money is your first priority, the only way you will succeed is if your only measure of success comes in the form of government-issued paper.

The Greatest Balancing Act on Earth

In the final analysis, the picture looks something like this:

That's right! As business people, you must become expert at balancing the needs of your business with your personal needs, your employees' needs, your shareholders' needs, your customers' and clients' needs, your family's needs, and your friends' needs.

Your values must lead you to build not only shareholder value, but also employee value, self-value, community value, and world value. Then and only then, I believe, can you begin to live the big business dream of becoming a great company.

➲ Practical and Tactical Advice ➲

For another perspective on what this new business model is about, consider these ideas from Stephen R. Covey's *The 8th Habit: From Effectiveness to Greatness.* They should tell you who truly embraces leading with the heart. If you work these suggestions into your business, you will be well on your way to *managing and leading with your heart.*

- Find your voice and inspire others to do the same.

- Find your voice in work that uses your talents, addresses your passion, and makes a difference in the world that is important to you.

- Practice leadership.

- Live, love, learn, contribute, and find meaning.

- Base your life on things such as fairness, kindness, respect, dignity, honesty, integrity, service, and giving.

- Be visionary, be disciplined, and be passionate.

- Be trustworthy and credible.

- Model, show the way, align, and empower.

- Be a servant-leader.

The Points to Ponder sprinkled throughout the book build on the key points in each chapter. Here's the first.

Points to Ponder

- This book is about change. It is about an environment where business leaders lead with the heart and thereby change the world in good and right ways.

- Be the change you wish to see in the world. Lead with your heart. Strive to create happiness for yourself and those you touch. Approach your mission with love, passion, commitment, and dedication. At the end of the day, measure success by the amount of happiness you leave in your wake. If you do, profits will be good.

- Hard work, structure, planning, and fiscal responsibility can be combined with happiness and wealth for all, without sacrificing the bottom line.

- Leading with your heart is not about being average, and it is not supportive of mediocrity or pain. It is about being the best you and your business can be.

- How many business people have the guts, know-how, vision, time, and financial wherewithal to create success, to lead with the heart, and to achieve a clear yet far-away vision?

(continued)

Points to Ponder *(concluded)*

- Lack of will and a never-say-die attitude are the only barriers to success for people who dream of a career in business and have the know-how to make it happen.

- Your success is tied to your values, ethics, and passion to grow your business in ways that make the world a better place.

- Build shareholder value, but also employee value, self-value, community value, and world value. Only then can you begin to live the big business dream of becoming a great company.

Blastoff!

If you think you are up to it, read on. If not, you already paid for the book—you might as well read on, too. You never know—you might be better at this then you think. I will share information that should make this balancing act much easier.

My best advice: Read on. Who knows? Your business may become the next Starbucks or Microsoft or GE. If you believe in yourself and what you're doing, all things are possible. If nothing else, I guarantee that you will find something within these pages to improve your enterprise and maybe yourself.

Chapter Two
The Right Stuff

Each of us must identify and understand our strengths and our weaknesses. We then can capitalize on our strengths and improve in those areas where we need to do better. We owe it to ourselves, our families, our employees, and our customers.

Do you really want to play in this game?

Managing and running a business is not for the weak of heart. This is a tough game played by all types of competitors, from the very nice to the not-so-nice to the plain-old-bad guy and gal. To be successful, you have to work with all kinds of people. Doing so can make you cynical, frustrated, fearful, angry, hateful, and sick.

Before becoming a manager, executive, or entrepreneur, look deep within yourself and ask these questions:

- Do I enjoy competition?
- Do I have *chutzpah*?
- Can I subvert my ego when called upon to do so?
- Am I patient?
- Can I accept criticism?
- Am I forgiving of myself and of others?
- Can I accept failure?
- Am I a good listener?
- Do I have a vision of where I want to go in life?
- Is my family supportive of that vision?

- Can I make sacrifices of time and money?
- Do I know my heart?
- Do I want those around me to be happy?
- Do I care about others?
- Do I want to lead with a heart?
- Do I have the right stuff?

These questions represent a good place to begin. If you answer no to any of them, management might not bring you happiness or wealth—it might steep you in a soup of unhappiness.

We all bring baggage to our work, but as long as we identify and accept our shortcomings, we can build or lead a business as bold and as strong as any. Most of us are just trying to have a great life, so we choose to build or manage the corner market with the best meatball sandwiches in the world or a software company that delivers what it promises and stands by the work.

Attributes Necessary for Success

Success and business growth revolve around these critical factors:

Credibility

Trust

Values

Keeping promises

Relationships and
partnerships

Brand development and
brand management

Business culture and
diversity

A focus on people first

Planning

Visionary thinking,
calculated risk taking,
and strategic thinking

Sales and marketing

Listening; solving and
meeting needs

Quality in everything you
produce and deliver

Customers expect us to deliver great products and great services. You cannot do less if you want to remain in business. Focus on those things that bring customers and clients to your door and drive long-term success.

Unfortunately, too many leaders focus on short-term earnings. As a result, they sacrifice value and quality by creating mediocre businesses and mediocre levels of customer service. These "leaders" don't really care much whether or not their investors, employees, customers, and neighbors receive much happiness from their business. If those leaders and their businesses went away tomorrow, you might not care or even notice.

When you build for the long-term, you build for greatness. Instead of focusing only on the bottom line, take a holistic business view and look always toward the future. Focus on people, not money. Recognize that business success is about Main Street, not Wall Street. Work hard to increase the happiness of all those people your business touches. This will result in great people-experiences and increased sales.

Look at the list of the critical factors again. Your greatness, your long-term success, your ability to lure the best and the brightest, and your commitment to your customers and clients all help to determine your bottom line and the prosperity and happiness of everyone you work with and serve.

As you work your way through the pages of the book, you will find practical advice to help you build your business. This chapter focuses on the keys to unlocking the heart and soul of any business. Heart and soul — not spreadsheets — are the core of every business. At least they should be.

Trust Equals Business Success.
Are you willing to build that trust?

Leading with your heart means first and foremost creating experiences that people believe are authentic — experiences they trust. Today's employees, customers and clients, potential customers and clients, and every person who is touched by a business enterprise in any way tend to be skeptical and not particularly trusting of corporations.

A December 2005 study by Datamonitor reported that 86 percent of the European and American consumers surveyed became more distrustful of business within the past five years.[1] Daniel Bone, Datamonitor's consumer analyst and author of the report, says that the primary causes for this breakdown in trust come from three main sources: A lack of business transparency; business complacency about winning customer trust and loyalty; and a decline in customer experience.

"The more positive experiences a consumer has with the brand, the more trustworthy he or she is likely to become," Bone writes.

Let's focus on the customer experience, the third of Bone's sources of distrust.

- When customers read about layoffs and then experience a decline in their experience, people conclude that efficiency and cutting costs are more important than customers.

- When customer service is outsourced overseas and customers perceive a decline in their experience, people conclude that efficiency and cutting costs are more important than customers.

- When customers read about CEOs making millions of dollars a year, while they bring home many times less, they conclude that no one person is that much more valuable to a business than any other person. Since employees are also consumers, they carry that perception over to other brands.

- When customers are over-sold or given a version of the truth, they conclude that sales are more important than consumers.

- And when all of the above perceptions are confirmed by business scandals, people's trust is broken.

In order to overcome consumer distrust, business leaders must start focusing their energy on the customer and the employee experience to create happiness. Businesses must build trust and credibility, create authentic experiences, and show in everything they say and do that they care more about people than they do profits.

As Bone says, "Brands are rooted in the trust that consumers place in them. After all, the ultimate goal of marketing is to generate an intense bond between the consumer and the brand, with trust being a fundamental factor in achieving this."

If you develop strong relationships based on values and trust, your business will benefit financially and your customers will begin the process of becoming loyal customers. This is the kind of long-term positive impact and payback that businesses strive to achieve.

⮕ Practical and Tactical Advice ⮔

Credibility, Trust, and Values

Do people believe what you say? Do you say what you mean? Is your business built on values that represent the heart and soul of its founders and leaders? Does the corporate culture buy into those values? And do the values represent core beliefs held by the executives and founders that reach beyond profit?

Truth, honesty, believability, and putting people above all else are the mainstays of developing positive feelings with others. Why would you expect anyone to buy your products or services if they cannot feel good about you as a caring human being? Even the much-maligned discount "big box" stores recognize this. We can debate how much they care, but we should not assume that they don't believe that spreading a caring message is one of the keys to long-term success. They do recognize that leading with the heart—or at least giving the appearance of doing so— is important to their shareholders.

The big-box stores argue that their low prices are based on value. They tell us that if they paid their employees better and improved their benefits, their customers would have to pay more for their products (and after all, they say, their low prices deliver happiness to their customers). Maybe they *are* being honest with themselves and us. They know what is inside their hearts—I cannot judge from where I sit. But whether or not their stores are reflective of their corporate values, they must know how important the concept is, or they wouldn't work so hard to claim their position.

If their customers, employees, and other stakeholders discover any insincerity in the values message, I believe the tremendous growth of big-box stores will plateau and we will witness another round of layoffs and closures from companies that misunderstand what leading with the heart looks and sounds like.

Little white lies and word games can lead to a breakdown in credibility. I believe strongly that we must all be 100 percent truthful 100 percent of the time. Sometimes that means turning down business because you know that you cannot deliver or because there is someone else who can deliver better. It is bitter medicine to swallow. Your business will prosper from the respect and credibility engendered by approaching your work with complete honesty, however.

Customers expect companies to do what's right for their customers, whether or not regulations require it. Do everything possible to exceed your customers' expectations if you want to earn their trust. To do that, you first must see the situation from the customer's perspective.

Trust can and must be built into everything you do with and for the customer or client. Every individual and department must do everything that is necessary to create this trust.

Business Relationships and Partnerships

What I am about to say is difficult for some to accept.

> **You do not sell products and services —
> you sell relationships and solutions.**

Everything you do must be for and about the customer. Your business must improve customers' lives in some way, it must do so consistently.

Your products and services must be as good as or better than the same or similar products and services offered by the other guy. Shoot for the highest quality, build that into the operation, make sure someone babysits quality control, and get on with building your business so that you can continue providing those great products and services.

Entrepreneurs, owners, presidents, principals, CEOs, COOs, and employees are all in the business of building relationships, and good relationships grow out of the credibility your business values and your brand engenders.

Building and Maintaining Relationships

Customers and clients do not generally come knocking on our doors out of nowhere. They are too busy running their own lives and/or businesses to be thinking about us. If you drive them to your door, you have a chance to make them happy, but if you want them to think of you first the next time they need what you offer, you had better do everything possible to succeed.

Great businesses spend great amounts of capital working to build and maintain ongoing business relationships and brand image. They do so because they believe strongly that everyone wants solid and trustworthy business relationships. They want to know that you care about them and want to understand their needs. They want to know that you are working hard to fulfill those needs. It's kind of like a marriage: You have to be attentive, sincere, reliable, dependable, trustworthy, and there *for them.*

Bain executives James Allen, Frederick F. Reichheld, and Barney Hamilton wrote about what customers think of their consumer experiences in 2005, reporting that about eighty percent of companies believed they delivered a superior customer experience, but only eight percent of their customers agreed with that assessment.

"The larger a company's market share, the greater the risk it will take its customers for granted. As the money flows in, management begins confusing customer profitability with customer loyalty, never realizing that the most lucrative buyers may also be the angriest and most alienated. Worse, traditional market research may lead the firm to view customers as statistics. Managers can become so focused on the data that they stop hearing the real voices of their customers," they said.

What's wrong with that picture? Based on those numbers, which likely haven't changed much since 2005, do most businesses deliver happiness? How much better and how much more profitable would they be if those numbers were reversed? Not listening and not measuring correctly can distort the value of customer loyalty. Measuring only for loyalty doesn't necessarily equal profitability, because customer loyalty is not always profitable.

Are customers profitable if they only purchase your product when you offer a sale or incentives? Are customers who purchase only low-margin products profitable? Are customers profitable if they hate their experience and your service but stay with you because you offer low prices or they are under contract? What if those same unhappy customers tell others how unhappy they are with you?

Savvy business people try to build loyalty in their most profitable customers and move their least profitable customers into that category by cross-selling and up-selling, and making sure that their customers are happy with them and are spreading the word.

How do we reverse the numbers so that 80 percent of customers believe they receive an exceptional customer experience? The Bain article provides a few clues.

1. Design the right offers and experiences for the right customers.

2. Deliver them by focusing the entire company on these offers and experiences.

3. Please customers again and again. Train employees and hold them accountable for the customer experience.

If you develop business relationships that are based on a plan and a commitment to please customers again and again, you will have return customers and new customers from referrals and leads.

Now *that's* what I call return on investment!

Business Culture

Disappointed customers and clients kill your brand and ultimately bury your business. When you promise one thing and deliver something inferior, you put the screws to your customers and clients. How many of those customers and clients will ever again purchase anything from your business? And what will disappointed, disrespected, and disdained customers and clients tell others about you? As a business person, I would rather stick my head in a hornet's nest than create such a situation.

Build a culture focused on honesty, trust, credibility, respect, dignity, and values, and hire only those people who share and manifest those values. Fire anyone who cannot adapt, because a culture armed against itself dooms your brand and your business.

When we make promises we know can't be kept (such as telling a customer that our product will do something it won't, or misrepresenting our earnings) we step into smelly stuff. Lying is unethical. It comes from greed and short-term thinking, and you know where that leads us: down the trail to betrayal and perhaps even federal prison. The greater harm isn't done to the customer, employee, or client (although that harm is great): The greater harm from unethical and illegal corporate behavior is that it creates a climate of distrust, dragging us and our institutions down.

Headlines and articles questioning business values harm us all. Not only do customers spend less time and money with us, but our quality is sabotaged because the best and the brightest will be disgusted enough to look for careers outside of business.

Researchers are learning that teenage girls believe business is boring and is driven by greed (usually represented by a focus on short-term earnings). Charlotte Shelton, a management professor at Rockhurst University in Kansas City, says, "The focus on short-term earnings is really destroying a lot of companies. It's turning them into cultures that nobody wants to work in."

A survey conducted by Simmons College School of Management and the Committee of 200 (a professional organization made up of women entrepreneurs and corporate leaders) of students in grades 7–12 revealed that only 15 percent of boys and 9 percent of girls between grades seven and 12 listed a business field as one of their top career choices. Try to imagine what this means for our businesses and for the greater good of society. It cannot be good news.

Great businesses thrive on diversity, creativity, and intelligence. Without bright people rushing to our enterprises, where will we get new and creative ideas, new and dynamic workplaces, and new and better products and services?

When you have large segments of society choosing not to work in business, small or large, entrepreneurial or corporate, businesses lose.

Points to Ponder

- Each of us must identify and understand our strengths and our weaknesses.

- Managing and running a business is not for the weak of heart.

- Success and business growth revolve around these critical factors:
  - Credibility
  - Trust
  - Values
  - Keeping promises
  - Relationships and partnerships
  - Brand development and brand management
  - Business culture and diversity
  - A focus on people
  - Planning
  - Visionary thinking, calculated risk taking, and strategic thinking
  - Sales and marketing
  - Listening; solving and meeting needs
  - Quality in everything you produce and deliver

(continued)

Points to Ponder *(concluded)*

- When we focus entirely on short-term earnings, we create mediocre businesses and mediocre levels of customer service.

- When we build for the long-term, we build for greatness.

- Entrepreneurs, owners, presidents, principals, CEOs, COOs, and employees are in the business of building relationships.

- Everything you do must be for and about the customer.

- Most companies believe they deliver a superior customer experience, but only a small percentage of customers agree.

Chapter Three
Building Your Business

Building a business requires more than a dream and hard work. Both are necessary ingredients for achieving success. But without strategic, planned, and disciplined growth, businesses usually fail to achieve their goals— assuming, of course, that they slow down along the way to *create* those goals.

Some enterprises manage to survive without measurable goals, aligned strategies, strategic planning, and business discipline, but seldom do they prosper, even when they build their foundation on strong values and lead with a heart. Happiness is a necessary ingredient if a business is to become great, but even happy employees cannot perform miracles when buffeted by bad planning, poor strategizing, and mediocre execution. Build your business with a heart, but practice smart and plan smart.

Fair warning: Plans alone do not guarantee success. And you cannot afford to spend vast amounts of time creating them—you have a business to run. If you do not have the expertise to build business and strategic plans, you should outsource the work. Larger businesses, start-up and established, likely will hire managers capable of completing the planning, and they will work in teams to accomplish the task. However the plans are done, execution targeted toward measurable goals equals success. Plans that sit on shelves or in desk drawers collecting dust are a complete waste of time, effort, and money.

Remember, success does not depend on planning; passionate, smart people can manage successfully. A business culture that strives for happiness thrives on good planning. As you develop your business and strategic plans, you should:

1. Reflect the passion inherent within the business.

2. Communicate that passion to every employee and to every customer, and to every potential customer.

3. Establish two or three stretch goals that are achievable; communicate those goals to everyone within the business; provide quarterly updates to everyone regarding progress in reaching the goals; and hold every department and every person in the business responsible and accountable for achieving the goals.

4. Engage every department and person by demanding that departmental goals serve to support the overall strategic plan.

5. Create a drop-dead deadline of one month for planning to be developed, approved, and communicated.

6. Create an integrated process through which the plan is launched, executed, and managed.

7. Finally, and perhaps most important, make sure the plans are not written in stone. Allow for quick left and right turns and new ideas.

Don't Drop That Dime

Before spending a dime on anything, managers, executives, and owners must make certain that every dime is being spent wisely; that investments in business development and growth offer potential return based on established margins and a targeted bottom line; and that the money works to achieve measurable goals.

In other words, build budgets after you create the business and strategic plans, and make sure that department heads and managers and those responsible for budgets aim every dollar at achieving the business's specific goals. And *then* launch the plans.

Business Plans

The smartest business leaders build their business plan before they open their doors. At a later date, you can revise the plan to raise capital or to make a left turn, if desired. Launching a business without a plan is not smart. However, don't despair if you neglected to develop a business plan. If your business breathes, there is time to build that critical plan for success.

No matter what size your business is, keep in mind that it takes capital to grow. If you plan to use your savings, your business plan had better be on target to make all that money back *plus* give you a substantial return on your investment (assuming, of course, that you enjoy having a roof over your head and eating regular meals).

If, on the other hand, you plan to raise capital from outside sources, understand that a reputable bank or investor won't invest in your business unless you have a well-thought-out business plan that proves you worthy of investment.

Seeking capital might not be an immediate objective, but business planning puts your train on the tracks and guides you toward greatness. And eventually, if you plan to grow and maximize your potential, you likely will need to raise monies.

Investors tell us that most business plans fail their tests. A surgeon doesn't operate on himself, and you shouldn't either. Business plans are complex. Hire someone skilled in the specific areas and content needed by your organization to build the plan. Hire a CPA, an attorney, and a business planner, or hire a business consultancy that understands investors and can manage each and every ingredient of a business plan, driving and executing it so that you reap the benefits of the consultancy's experience and talents.

If you are not a CPA, not an attorney, not a marketer, not a sales person, not a market researcher, and not a visionary all wrapped up in one body, I urge you to use experts to help build your plan. If you are setting up a board of directors, seek directors who have some of the necessary skills in addition to deep pockets. Furthermore, be sure the people on your board possess the values on which your business is being built. If happiness is important to you, it had better be important to your directors as well, or there will be trouble.

When you lead with your heart and strive to put people first, your first step in building the plan is to identify the values on which the company will run. These values must represent the true and authentic values of every owner and founder of the business. If your business is built correctly, everything that follows will align with these values. The values should be printed on business plans, organizational strategic plans, and departmental strategic plans.

Strategic Plans

The purpose of a strategic plan is to create a road map for where your business is going. In brief, the organizational strategic plan should spell out the following:

1. **Objective** (what you want to achieve).

2. **Goals** (What does success look like? What goals must be met to achieve the objective?). Keep these to two or three goals per year, and make sure they are measurable. Measure progress quarterly, and share those results with every employee. If you wait until the end of the year to analyze the plan's success, it will be too late to adjust the plan to achieve the objective.

3. **Strategies** (what you will do to achieve the goals).

4. **Tactics** (how you will achieve the strategies). Tactics are tools such as advertising, marketing, public relations, and sales.

Every goal, strategy, and tactic must be measurable and measured at least quarterly, and then revised if necessary to achieve the goals.

Organizational and departmental strategic plans should be done annually. Product plans should be done for every product launch or re-launch. Do the organizational plan first, so that department and functional area plans focus on achieving the organization's objectives and goals. Experienced and knowledgeable strategic thinkers who know how to plan and execute the actions for strategic success should be able to create the plan in a cost-effective and efficient manner in-house. If those kinds of managers and executives are not available to build the plan, a good business consultant can help.

Departmental heads and functional area leaders should then design their plans to support and achieve the company's objectives and goals. Budgets are tied to departmental needs to achieve the goals, not based on nice-to-have-or-do budget items. Once the organization's strategic plan is completed, it should be shared with and explained to every employee so that everyone in the company is aligned and working to achieve the goals.

Business Discipline Focused on Ethics and Values

Is there anything more useless than plans sitting on shelves, or more frustrating to those who sweated over every detail, trying to create a document worthy of business success?

Businesses achieve greatness because their leaders and employees are passionate, engaged, and customer-focused. Planning regularly and then making sure that every plan lives by measurement, analysis, and change provides structure for the passion to reach your audiences. Every quarter, you should analyze the results of your planning; share both the good and the bad with every employee; revise strategies and tactics when necessary; and drive toward the goals and objective. This work represents the management and execution of the plan. Without management and execution, a plan is dead on arrival.

Business discipline begins and ends at the top, and for plans to succeed, discipline must be applied to everything you do. Even the smallest of businesses can succeed if they plan for success by aligning every function and every person with that plan, measuring regularly throughout the life of the plan, and holding every person (even if it is just yourself) accountable for achieving the goals and objectives. If the business is built on values and truly focuses on customers, the strategic plan and the business plan will be built on decisions that have been strained through the filters of the company's values. Every tactic will be designed to please customers, and every member of the company will be motivated to please the customer because they will be chosen based not only on their résumés, but also on their values. Every member of the organization will be aligned within the culture—they will fit perfectly, forming a complete yet complex business puzzle that is beautiful to see.

In organizations like this, employees are proud of the work they do and proud of the company they belong to. They derive pleasure from the company's success. They believe in what they do, they believe that their work produces good, and they believe their products and services are beneficial. They believe all this because it is true—not because executives say so or because they receive great wages and benefits.

So, how does a leader know if his or her company is values-based?

During his tenure as chairman of the U.S. Securities and Exchange Commission, William Donaldson emphasized the importance of corporate ethics. He encouraged leaders to ask questions about their cultures, such as these:

- What kind of moral compass do you want guiding this corporation?

- What ethical standards do you want embedded in this corporation's DNA?

- And how will you demonstrate it in your every action?

In 2004, the U.S. Sentencing Commission urged companies to promote organizational cultures that encourage ethical conduct and commit to compliance with the law.

Clearly, you have a mandate to create values-based workplaces.

Curtis C. Verschoor wrote an article about business ethics in which he called for business leaders to restore public and investor trust in business by creating environments that can lead businesses to greatness. Verschoor outlined his recommendations in an article for internal auditors, but I believe that those recommendations are just as relevant to business leaders. The corporate environment he recommends would be characterized by:

- Promoting good business through technology and ethics
- Integrity
- Accountability and personal responsibility
- Risk-taking
- Learning from our mistakes
- Being the best we can be
- Collaboration

In addition to internal audits, Verschoor recommends that businesses survey their employees about the values inherent within the workplace and ask whether or not they feel that leadership demands and supports a values-based culture. He also suggests that the organization's personnel practices be analyzed to determine whether or not they help employees contribute to a positive corporate ethical climate.

I cannot stress enough that whether you run a one-person shop or you run a 100,000-person business, values are integral to creating a productive and prosperous work environment that scores high with employees and customers on happiness.

Where's the Passion?

The final ingredient sets a few businesses apart from all others. In fact, some believe that it represents the master key to greatness. What is it? *Passion*. Without it, businesses seldom separate themselves from the pack.

Unfortunately, passion is not something learned or purchased. Either business leaders have it and spread it throughout their company culture, or they don't.

Employees have it because they believe in what they do, or they don't. Customers have it because they trust the company, or they don't.

➲ Practical and Tactical Advice ➫

Smart planning and execution ensure that employee passion and values stir the pot throughout the organization, making a great soup spiced with benefits for customers.

To inspire passion, here are a few recommendations:

1. Hire only those people who share your passion and your values. If you err in hiring, help those who do not fit the culture to find work elsewhere.

2. Establish quarterly and measurable organizational goals. Make sure that every employee knows what the goals are and is committed to achieving them. It takes the entire organization to achieve success! One weak link negatively affects the bottom line, and hurts morale, productivity, and your culture.

3. Tie employee compensation to achieving organizational goals. Every person, from top to bottom, needs to be held accountable for success *and* rewarded when your business achieves its goals.

4. Have fun! That's right, create an environment where people are not only challenged by their work, but also enjoy the organization. Celebrate birthdays and anniversaries, recognize individuals and teams for outstanding contributions, and throw the occasional

party. I guarantee that your company's bottom line will improve and passion will flow like an excellent Italian sauce — hot and impossible to ignore.

Points to Ponder

- Without strategic, planned, and disciplined growth, your business will not be the best it can be.

- Happiness is a necessary ingredient for greatness.

- Develop a business plan before you launch your business.

- Your first step in creating the plan is to identify the values on which the company will run.

- Businesses achieve greatness because they plan regularly and they make sure that every plan is measured, analyzed, and changed at least annually.

- Without passion, it is very hard to separate yourself from the pack.

Chapter Four
Building a Powerful Brand

Before we discuss how to create a business plan, we need to discuss your Brand, spelled with a capital B. No matter what your business does and how it works, current and potential customers and clients will create a mental image or perception of your business. That perception is your Brand image. Customer perception of your business will ultimately determine any and all levels of success that you will achieve. We discuss it now because your business plan and all of your strategic plans need to incorporate the driving forces that build a great Brand image.

If your Brand is not authentic (from the heart and true to your values) and focused completely on people, your Brand likely will be spelled with a little "b": few people will be passionate about and engaged with your products and services or your business image. And you won't get noticed.

Everything your business does or says determines what your Brand looks like in the public's eye, and helps determine whether or not the public will purchase your products or services. Your employees are the face of your Brand, and are the most important part of your business. Therefore, your Brand must be built first with your employees.

Employees "touch" customers and clients in very personal ways, whether they work in the call center, in the marketing department, or on the plant floor. They communicate with customers, they make the products or furnish the services, and they build the company's image. The way customers perceive your business is directly related to the quality of the contact they have with your employees. If you do not lead your employees from your heart, using values as your backbone and happiness as your soul, your Brand will suffer—business succeeds or fails on the back of your company's Brand. If employees are not passionate and engaged, why should your customers be passionate and engaged? To be the best you can be, here are the top five areas, in order of importance, where you must focus most of your attention:

1. Employees
2. Customers
3. All stakeholders (including employees and customers)
4. Your hiring practices
5. Potential customers

I want to share two personal experiences that provide simple examples of the face of a Brand—the first positive, the second negative.

I once worked at Starbucks as manager of internal communications. One day I received a call from a vice president in retail. He told me about a store employee who tattooed the Starbucks logo on his arm. Never one to resist a good story, I asked the editor of our newsletter to get the details.

In the next issue, we ran the employee's picture in which he prominently displayed his tattooed logo, accompanied by a brief article explaining why an otherwise sane and smart person would do such a thing. It was quite simple: He loved Starbucks — he loved his job, he loved the coffee, he loved his co-workers, and he loved the customers. His happiness was off the charts, and with his passion for the company, its products, and its services, he was creating a positive Brand image.

And now the second story. On a cold Sunday morning, I stopped at a Starbucks store on Queen Anne Hill in Seattle with my wife and several friends to get coffee and something to eat. I overheard one barista tell a colleague that this was his last shift and that he could not wait for it to end so that he could leave Starbucks and get on with his life. Imagine the impression he left with those who visited that day. The store manager and the district manager should have let him go as soon as he gave his notice and paid him for the next two weeks. Brands suffer when employees exhibit bad attitudes.

Nearly all interactions with Starbucks employees produce a positive reaction to the Brand because they exhibit passion for what they do. This does not happen by accident. Candidates for employment are given a kind of "values" test to see if they are a good fit for the culture before they are hired. (Some bad seeds are not filtered out, of course, because no system is flawless.) And then they are treated to regular culture training and product and service training. Is it any wonder that Starbucks boasts one of the most recognizable brands in the world, and has in 10 years grown from a multi-million dollar business to a multi-billion dollar business? Starbucks combines values, happiness, and business sense to generate the passion people feel about its Brand.

Customers and employees base their perception of your business on the quality of their human contacts with your company, not on the quality of your services and products (which they expect to be good or great. If products or services don't meet customer expectations, the only direction your brand image can go is down). Therefore, every person working within your business, every communication created, and everything you do represents and determines your Brand image.

According to Accenture's 2005 annual survey, top executives understand the importance of building the Brand from the inside out. Strengthening their organization's human capital is the number-one issue among the top executives surveyed. Approximately 33 percent said that changing their organization's culture and changing employee attitudes are their top-of-mind concern. They know that their business and their Brand rest on the shoulders of their people. What those people say and do — the values they declare verbally and through their body language — are key to their company's Brand image.

At great companies, employees are hired based on the likelihood that they will fit comfortably within the existing culture. And then they receive hours of training to help them succeed, followed by frequent and consistent communication about their company's Brand and what it represents. I believe that this internal focus drives success more than any other factor.

Brand Infatuation

John Gaffney wrote about this very subject in *1to1 Magazine.* "There are some very fortunate companies whose logos, brands, products, and services have achieved iconic status," he wrote. "Harley-Davidson is certainly one of them. So is Corvette. And Mustang. You can also put Virgin, the NFL, Starbucks, Coke, Intel, FedEx, Microsoft, Nike, and the Rolling Stones into the engaged category. These brands have not only inspired, but have created powerfully tight relationships with their customers. The process and strategies behind these 'superbrands' have spawned a new area of thinking in customer strategy: customer engagement."

"Engagement," Gaffney explains, "is the difference between a changeable relationship and an intense bond. It is a powerful tool for altering customer behavior and adding to the value of a customer base. An engaged customer will buy a $200 Coach bag on a salary better suited for a $30 one from Gap."

I don't think a $200 Coach bag vs. a $30 bag has anything to do with personal happiness. However, taking Gaffney's point regarding "engagement" makes me believe that the company selling the $200 bag is doing something right— they are engaging the customer. And engaged customers can add value to a customer base. I would argue, however, that simply purchasing the $200 bag might not mean that the Brand creates the kind of passion necessary to maximize potential of your business or to create a great Brand. However, I include his point about engagement because it is an important one.

Gaffney identifies five elements of customer engagement. They are:

1. Identification   4. Aspiration
2. Recommendation   5. Anticipation
3. Experience

Gaffney concludes, "The brand is a promise; a company creates customer engagement when it fulfills that promise and incorporates identification, recommendation, experience, aspiration, and anticipation into its customer strategy. And if the company does it right, maybe its customers will dress their dog in its merchandise or tattoo its logo on their arms."

When those things come together for customers and when employees create those types of experiences, businesses achieve a happiness that results in great companies and great brands.

In their book *Best Face Forward*, Jeffrey Rayport and Bernard Jaworkski argue, "The quality of interactions with customers — and the customer experiences that result from those interactions — is rapidly becoming the sole remaining basis of competitive advantage."

With all the available evidence, why don't all companies focus on creating a culture in which employees take great pride in what they do because they are trained and respected and rewarded by leaders who practice honesty and openness and who believe that brands are created from the inside out? If they did, they would have customers who couldn't wait to try the experience, and current customers who would return again and again.

The problem is that too many companies don't know their customers. A 2005 Forrester survey of corporate decision makers reveals that most companies fail to consider the needs of target customers in their decision making and fail to take the time to monitor the quality of customer interactions. And according to a study by the Strativity Group, a majority of senior executives do not know the average annual value of a customer or even the cost of resolving a complaint.[1]

The information I present next is so good that I am compelled to share it with you. It is a list of 10 rules that come from Simon Williams, chairman of the New York-based branding consultancy Sterling Group. Simon Williams encourages this sharing, so I urge you to share these tips with your staffs.

Simon Williams's
10 New Rules of Branding

1. Brands that influence culture sell more; culture is the new catalyst for growth. "Look at Google. They are changing the way you behave online," Williams says. "Nike is a brand that has become a part of all culture. If you get into that split screen, you become part of the lexicon of life."

2. A brand with no point of view has no point; full-flavor branding is in, vanilla is out. "Love or hate Fox News, you know where it stands on issues," Williams points out. "And Ben & Jerry's is more than just ice cream; it's a company that stands for a cause. Younger consumers have grown up in a consumer world. They're flexing their muscle, and they want their brands to stand for something."

3. Today's consumer is leading from the front; this is the smartest generation to have ever walked the planet. "Today's consumers have very strong opinions on brands, and a lot of brands are getting consumers involved," Williams says. "Take Converse and the Converse Gallery, where consumers can make a 24-second film that will run on their site. It is consumer-generated creativity and a natural savviness."

4. Customize wherever and whenever you can; customization is tomorrow's killer whale. "Consumers say, 'I need something that is mine, not mass-produced for everybody.'" He points to brands such as Apple's iTunes Web site, where consumers buy the tracks they want and place them on their iPods; Starbucks, which creates beverages consumers want; and Nike, which allows you to design shoes online.

(continued)

The 10 New Rules of Branding *(concluded)*

5. Forget the transaction—just give me an experience. The mandate is simple: Wow them every day, every way. Williams says that the best way to give consumers a brand experience is to provide an entire experience.

6. Deliver clarity at point of purchase; be obsessive about presentation. "If I'm a consumer and I stand in front of a shelf, I see a wall of product. Brands are beginning to recognize that you have to be clear about what they are selling at the point of purchase."

7. You are only as good as your weakest link. Do you know where you're vulnerable? There is zero tolerance for a brand that makes a mistake. "Brands like Wal-Mart and Nike are still connected to negative PR about alleged abuse of foreign workers," explains Williams.

8. Social responsibility is no longer an option. What's your cause? What's your contribution? Consumers expect companies to generate cause marketing.

9. Pulse, pace, and passion really make a difference. Had your heartbeat checked recently? "You're in a crazy world. You keep piling more devices upon us. The more you have, the more you need. If your business does not have a high metabolic rate, you're not going to survive. Companies like Google move fast, and that means the older, slower companies are doomed."

10. Innovation is the new boardroom favorite. "Brands are inspired by Apple more than anyone else. They transformed the music business, and people are taking what they did seriously. Procter & Gamble and GE are driving this and have made innovation the core of their corporate strategy."

Make Success a Part of Your Plan

Business success is no accident. Business leaders who achieve their goals and create companies that become great and lasting have something in common: They plan for it. They are visionary. They build an organization based on values. They believe their Brand is more important than a product or a service.

Great companies build great products and sell great services. Their leaders, their employees, and their customers expect nothing less. But not all these leaders and employees who make great products and offer great services build great Brands. Great Brands arise from visionary companies built on values, credibility, and trust. And companies with leaders who lead from the heart and care about happiness lead from the front.

To that end, great executives and business owners build their Brand not only by jumping on the next great product or idea—they build it from the inside out. (If they do it right.)

The 3M Company created what it calls a "15 percent rule." Employees are encouraged to spend up to 15 percent of their time on their ideas and projects. Art Fry used the rule to co-invent, to develop, and to launch Post-it Notes.

It seems that Fry used to insert tiny pieces of paper into his hymnal at church so he could quickly locate that Sunday's songs. Unfortunately, the papers usually fell to the floor. He thought about how it would be more efficient if he could add a bit of adhesive to one end of the paper. So he looked up fellow 3M employee Spence Silver, who had invented an adhesive, and together, they created Post-it Notes. The rest is business hall-of-fame history.

None of this would have been possible without a culture that encourages employees to try things, a culture where employees are given the power to fail or succeed and are encouraged to take risks. You see, at companies like 3M, leaders believe that you often get to where you are going by making mistakes—and you can't make mistakes if you aren't trying new things. This is an example of building from the inside-out. Post-it Notes didn't grow out of an executive's mind or an R&D lab's great idea. It wasn't top-down and it didn't come out of market research. It came from the bottom up, and I am willing to bet that Fry and Silver experienced a happiness high. Millions of us cannot imagine life without Post-it Notes. That little invention makes us happy day after day, and 3M's Brand experiences greatness because of a thousand stories just like this one.

In this information age, consumers tend to assume that a product or service will deliver what you say it will. And they know what you say about it because of technology and exposure to marketing. The question we must all answer is this: With most things being relatively equal, including price, why should they select your product or service over your competitor's?

The answer? They select or reject it based on their perception of your Brand. And differentiation (or the consumer's perception) between you and others grows out of your Brand image, which is built on your values, vision, credibility, trust, and happiness.

It is these traits—values, vision, credibility, trust, and happiness—that create perception in the consumer's mind. If they believe you are great, then you are. Therefore, your strategic and business planning must be designed to build the Brand as well as to increase sales and margins.

Here is an example of what a company's values or guiding principles might look like:

Core Purpose

To provide services and the best professional specialists available to grow clients' businesses, while enhancing their happiness.

Core Values

1. We treat every person with respect and dignity.

2. We promise always to place trust, credibility, honesty, and integrity above profits.

3. We only take on clients for whom we can make a difference and help its business grow.

4. We give back to the community by offering our services pro bono to organizations and institutions deemed suitable and appropriate.

5. We commit to enhancing working environments and natural environments.

➲ Practical and Tactical Advice ➲

"The purpose of a business is to create a customer," Peter Drucker says. I would add that the purpose of any strategic plan is to move potential customers and clients to ring the register. Until that register rings, our business resembles an unpublished writer—merely a wannabe. Without a plan to show us where you are going, you might as well be flying in the Bermuda Triangle, waiting to hit the water below and then go forever missing from the world.

I cannot stress it often enough: Planning is one of the keys to business success. If you do it correctly, you will grow because you will have distinguished yourself from your competitors. Unplanned, undisciplined, and unstructured growth will cause you to crash and burn. Careful and well-thought-out planning creates a road map to success.

The Keys to the Road Map

Every plan is driven by a purpose, as well as by goals and a target market, and it has to be customized to meet the business's needs. Successful planning and brand building depend on seven main components:

- **The Business Plan**

- **A Core Purpose:** The reason why your company exists, beyond just making money.

- **Core Values:** The values of the founders and leaders of the business. If any of these values go away, the business as it is would cease to exist. These values do not usually include making a profit, but there are great companies that consider profit a value and explain that profits are necessary to stay in business, to do good, and so on. (I personally don't believe that it is a good idea to include making profits as a value—it should be obvious that you won't exist if your business does not make a profit.)

  Again, I turn to Collins and Porras for a definition: "The organization's essential and enduring tenets—a small set of general guiding principles—not to be confused with specific cultural or operating practices, not to be compromised for financial gain or short-term expediency."

In Collins's and Porras's research, they learned that the greatest companies, as measured by CEOs, had one thing in common—they all took the time to state their values, and they lived by those values. It is what distinguishes the great from the good, the bad, and the dead.

- **A Vision:** This is not a number or a goal. For a definition, I again turn to Jim Collins and Jerry Porras: "Enduring and successful corporations . . . distinguish their timeless core values and enduring core purpose (which should never change) from their operating practices and business strategies (which should be changed constantly in response to a changing world). . . . A well-conceived vision consists of two major components—core ideology (made up of core values and core purpose) and an envisioned future (a 10 to 30 year goal . . . and a vivid description of what that goal looks like)."

- **A Long-Term Goal** that energizes employees and is clear and precise, such as that of

  - *GE:* "To become #1 or #2 in every market you serve and revolutionize this company to have the speed and agility of a small enterprise."
  - *Starbucks:* "To become the most recognized brand in the world."

- **A Mission or Vision Statement:** What your company will look like in 10, 15, 20, 25, or 30 years.

— Here is another example of what these statements might look like:

Mission

The Company will offer business solutions delivered by the best available business professionals at competitive rates that deliver value and return on investment to every client.

Vision

To become the most respected consulting firm in the United States.

Twenty-five-year Goal

To be the most recognizable, desirable, and sought-after business solutions enterprise in the United States.

E-mail Sabotage: Killing the Brand Softly

We live in an e-world where Web and e-tools are becoming more important. They will be used more and more by your customers and your employees. Stop and think before you delete! If you don't, you risk killing your brand and ultimately your business. In today's marketplace, ignoring the e-mail inbox could shorten your business lifespan by killing your brand image.

Think about it: Would you intentionally ignore your clients and send messages saying that you don't care about them or their business? That is exactly what you do when you ignore e-mail or respond slowly or inaccurately.

Brand image is built from the inside out. Every communication that takes place between a company and a customer, a potential customer, a vendor, a business, and even a competitor results in a positive or a negative impression. And when those impressions are added together, they make up brand image.

Your brand image is the lifeblood of your business. It must reflect near perfection if you expect others to trust your expertise and to want your products and services. Furthermore, you need to make certain that your employees understand the dangers of messy e-mail communications.

A recent survey of the retail industry conducted by Benchmark Portal and sponsored by eGain Communications Corp. tells the tale of what looks like a trend in the business world. The numbers indicate that most businesses are in a lot of trouble when it comes to their "customer e-service." Twenty-six percent of retailers surveyed failed to respond to e-mail inquiries from customers seeking to make a purchase. Forty-seven percent of retailers, for example, fail to respond to customer e-mails within 24 hours, compared to a rate of only 61 percent for all industries. [2]

Conducted in July of 2005, the survey found that of those companies that do respond to client or customer e-mails, about 35 percent of retailers sent e-mails rated by Benchmark Portal as "good" at answering customers' questions, while a sad 17 percent of all industries were rated good. Twenty-eight percent of retailers sent e-mails rated "fair," compared to 26 percent of all industries; Nine percent of retailers sent "poor" e-mails, compared to the cross-industry rate of 14 percent.

Another survey conducted by *Internet Retailer* in February of 2007 summarized its results this way: "When it comes to customer service, online shoppers above all else want consistency. If a call or e-mail goes unanswered or a service rep can't help a shopper track a package, customers will vote with their pocketbooks and take their business elsewhere." [3]

The numbers show that among all respondents, 18.4 percent take more than eight hours to respond but 9.4 percent don't know how long it takes them to respond to customer e-mails.

Online journal *eMarketer*'s senior analyst David Hallerman also recently surveyed the state of business e-mail marketing, reporting that turnaround time for e-mail sent to top firms is getting longer. His survey revealed that only a modest percentage of responding companies respond to customer e-mails within 24 hours. Only 50% of the responding firms said that they answer their customer e-mail!

Businesses cannot afford to ignore those numbers, even if only a tiny percentage of these e-mails fall into the commercial category. Alienating even one client hurts brand image and eventually sales. Alienating hundreds, thousands, or tens of thousands of e-mailers over the life of a business can therefore be deadly. Brand image is all about client perception. Sales will drop, but what's worse is that you open the door to competitors who do give e-mail and every other communication channel the constant attention it needs.

Some managers do not understand the damage that is done by failing to respond or by badly responding to e-mail. Business leaders must recognize this before a serious crisis erupts and it's too late. In our pervasively online technological age, shoppers, customers, clients, vendors, and competitors are choosing e-mail more and more as their preferred communication tool. Furthermore, study results suggest that businesses miss up to two-thirds of their potential audience because they do not add e-mail to their marketing tool kit.

E-mail Tips

Here are a few tips for turning e-mail into a business tool rather than a coupon for business suicide:

1. Respond accurately to all e-mails with 24 hours.

2. Embrace e-mail as a marketing tool.

3. Use SPAM filters if necessary (but only if necessary) to block e-mails originating from spammers, but do so *cautiously*. Blocking e-mails from legitimate clients and others will hurt your business in the long run.

4. For best results and greatest returns on investment, customize outgoing e-mail messages by employing some kind of consolidated client and prospect database that allows you to specifically identify client groups' needs, wants, and desires.

5. Communicate customized messages that meet the needs, wants, and desires of those client groups.

Businesses that follow these practices bask in results-oriented e-mail marketing and brand building. Home Depot, for example, has grown its client e-mail database from 500,000 to five million contacts in just the last two years. Each one of these five million e-mail addresses represents solid future sales.

By embracing e-mail, you can grow sales by melding ingredients gleaned from its customer data points and then managing them so as to collect the right data and create the right message from the right sender through the right channel at the right times. Customers and clients count. They measure your value and develop a perception around that value. By ignoring e-mail or using it ineffectively, you miss countless opportunities to create positive customer perceptions. This shortens your business's lifespan. Treating e-mail like the winning tool it can be, however, holds the potential of extending your business's lifespan (and profits) indefinitely.

Constant Change

Malcolm Gladwell, author of the best-selling book *The Tipping Point,* believes that the next social epidemic will be the exodus of Baby Boomers from the workforce, and that companies having strong relationships with their Generation X workers (defined here as those born between 1961 and 1981) will thrive.

This is important to those of us who believe that you build brands from the inside out. You must understand the needs of your employees if you are to build strong cultures that interpret and pass on the brand image appropriately. In addition to Generation X, you must also understand Generation Y and the Millennial Generation to succeed in your business. Members of these generations will be making up most of your customers and your employees in the future.

For the sake of the brand and your business health, start thinking about creating an X-, Y-, and Millennium-friendly workplace, so that the generational transition is smooth.

Boston Globe columnist Penelope Trunk writes in her new book *Brazen Careerist: The New Rules for Success* that "Young employees today are breaking new ground in the business world and searching for fresh way to reach their career goals on their own terms . . . without necessarily climbing the corporate ladder."

She predicts six workplace trends:

1. The end of gender-based pay disparity.
2. The end of the glass ceiling.
3. The end of the work grind.
4. The end of consulting (because all workers will feel like consultants , thus rendering the term useless).
5. The end of the stay-at-home parent, as men and women will all seek flexible job schedules so they can raise their children.
6. The end of hierarchy.

The message: Never assume that you know all the needs of your workers or your customers. To succeed, you must make every effort to understand and respond to those needs, which are ever-changing within and between generations.

Looking Forward with Our Planning

In his book *The Five Keys to Branding Success in 2006,* Dr. Robert Passikoff suggests that we need to understand consumer values 12–18 months in advance." [4]

He identified five leading indicators that would predict the future of brands in 2006, but the list can help you predict trends as you plan today. I selected three of his indicators that I believe you must focus on:

1. How do advertising and marketing increase your brand's strength in the eyes of the consumers and predicts sales and profitability?

2. How will your Web sites and high-tech capabilities accommodate your customer's wants and needs, and differentiate you from your competition?

3. How will you increase and measure your Web site and technology potential?

You need to use forward-looking and predictive analysis in your business, whether or not it grows out of your own research or comes from a reliable outside source, because you always need to be forward looking.

Points to Ponder

- Customers and clients have a perception of your business. This is your brand image.

- If you are not passionate about your products and services or your business image, others won't be, either.

- Employees are the face of your brand. Therefore, your employees are the most important part of your business.

- Your business succeeds or fails on the back of your Brand.

- The quality of interactions with customers is rapidly becoming the sole remaining basis of competitive advantage.

- Business leaders who achieve their goals and create companies that become great plan for it. They build an organization based on values, and they believe their Brand is more important than a product or a service.

- Never assume that you know the needs of your workers or your customers.

Chapter Five
The Business Plan

Don't skip this chapter. If you already have a business plan, you might need to go back and rethink some of your original ideas after reading what follows. It's okay to pour new concrete where there are cracks in your foundation.

Entire books are written on this subject. I provide the basics so that you will understand what a business plan looks like. Unless you are an expert, you will need to hire a consulting firm or individual experts to create your business plan. This chapter will get you started on the process.

If you haven't already created a business plan and you think your business is doing just fine, shame on you. Your business will do much better if you develop one, even though you are months or even years late in doing so. And if you are an entrepreneur getting ready to launch a new business, congratulations! You have come to the right station for the train to success. Just remember: You are the engineer, not me. And you must handle execution carefully, if you don't want to slide off the tracks.

Keep in mind that we are discussing a different kind of business model—a model that centers on people, happiness, and great experiences. As you read on, try to imagine the kinds of employees, customers, and clients that you will involve or hire to build a people-centered culture in which everyone pitches in to create great experiences for customers and employees who are passionate about the business and engaged in its success. And then create a plan designed to bring them the happiness they deserve and want. If you put all that in your business plan, you will decrease your chances of future disasters that require drastic cost-cutting, down_ sizing, and even re-engineering. Build it right the first time and you will be able to move forward, based on your plan's goals. Be warned: You will make lots of unexpected lefts and rights. That's good if it reflects changes that get you to where you want to go better, faster, and cheaper.

Change is inevitable; reversals of fortune are not. Good planning followed by exceptional execution leads to more good than bad. If you are both good and lucky, maybe you won't have bad experiences. But be realistic. Surround yourself with smart people who fit the kind of culture necessary for your success. Always think of people first. Develop authentic and heart-felt values. Filter every decision through your values. Always strive to raise the level of your business's happiness. Do these things and your Brand will engender loyalty and passion, and your earnings chart will show many more ups than downs.

Creating the Successful Business Plan

I don't believe any business should hang out its "open for business" sign until it has created a business plan. Most of us don't go to the grocery store without some kind of plan—even if it is as simple as remembering to buy milk because tomorrow's cereal will be dry and tasteless if we don't go to the store today.

Why fail to plan before making a life-changing decision that promises to impact your future and your employees' futures like very little else in life? Without a plan to achieve success, you are skydiving without a parachute.

Yet so many businesses do just that. The result is some level of failure, or at the very least, a level of success that could be far greater if a plan was carefully crafted first. Some people do survive without parachutes, but hitting the ground isn't much fun, so why do it?

What is a Business Plan?

Staying within my philosophy of keeping things as simple as possible, allow me to borrow a definition of "business plan" from investorwords.com, an online investor glossary:

> "A document prepared by a company's management, detailing the past, present, and future of the company, usually designed to attract capital investment."

This is an excellent definition, but I believe that we not only write a business plan to sell the business concept or to raise monies, but also to create a business built on a firm foundation. The building sits atop concrete that has been poured carefully and bricks that are laid with great care to form a structure that will withstand changes in the weather and fluctuations in the climate. And every business person knows that fluctuations in the climate happen, and often without warning. The business plan and your strategic plans help you stay safe in bad weather.

Don't focus on money—focus on people.

Happiness has to do with meeting people's wants, needs, and desires, which may or may not tickle their emotional sides 24/7. It is about a lot more than feel-good emotions and simple satisfaction. Even if we wanted to, we cannot control people's emotions. Happiness is about first understanding what motivates and inspires people to become loyal to a brand, and then using that information to build an internal and an external culture of brand advocates who believe in and strive to always exceed human expectations.

To be successful, we must build from the inside out. This means having a carefully structured strategic plan that is flexible and includes measurable goals. It must reflect the input from every department. Every employee must be held accountable for achieving the goals.

Creating happiness among our employees and customers starts at the beginning:

Creating Happiness

1. The Business Plan and the business's core values must be based on happiness and long-term revenue success (not short-term).

2. The business's core purpose must reflect something other than making money.

3. The annual Strategic Plan recognizes that:

   a. Employees at every level must participate in building the plan.
   b. They must be responsible and accountable for achieving the plan.
   c. The goals must be measured in terms of exceeding employee and customer wants, needs, and desires.
   d. The goals must be progressive and must not be about Wall Street—always about Main Street. Evidence supports the fact that companies that operate in this way usually exceed the median expectations of Wall Street.

4. From the beginning, every employee must be focused on building a culture true to the business's core values.

5. Every business decision must be filtered through the core values.

6. Every employee must receive ongoing brand and values training.

7. Every employee must receive ongoing and honest internal communication. The good and the bad must be shared.

8. Every employee must receive encouragement and have access to a structure that enables risk-taking and innovation.

9. Every employee must be held responsible and accountable for both internal and external marketing and brand-building.

10. Employees and customers must be honored, recognized, and rewarded for suggestions, ideas, and innovations that make the company better.

At the end of the day, it is always about the "who," not the "what." It is about people, not revenues. When it is about people, the revenues will come.

First Steps

Few business people are able to answer the obvious questions:

- What does your business do?
- What does your culture look like?
- Who are your customers?

Far too many executives, owners, and partners answer this way: "We sell widgets, we have hardworking employees who make them, and everyone who needs widgets is our customer." Wrong!

You might sell widgets, your employees might be hard-working, and everyone who needs widgets might be a potential customer, but that is not your business's core purpose. And not everyone who needs a widget is or will become your customer.

Let me explain. In today's marketplace, customers are more savvy and aware of their needs than ever before. They know what they want, when they want it, and often where to get it. And if they need a widget, they probably know what specific kind of widget they need and how much they are willing to pay for it.

More important to the business person, however, is the understanding that even those needing widgets aren't buying just widgets—they are buying solutions. Nobody buys a widget just to keep it around the shop or the house—they buy a widget to solve some sort of challenge or problem or need.

So, if you sell widgets instead of solutions, you become simply a tree in a large forest. On the other hand, if you provide solutions or experiences or things that uniquely meet your customer's needs or values that can't be found anywhere else, then you become a refreshing brook running through the forest that provides sustenance to the trees—in this example, your customers' trees. Which would you rather be: A tree among many trees, or the brook that feeds the trees?

And what kind of customer would you rather have: a customer who is looking for any old tree, or a customer who is seeking the brook?

And who will be the happier customer: the one buying a widget, or the one buying the solution?

And who makes a better return customer: the purchaser of a widget, or the happy customer whose problem or need you solved?

Here is another way to look at this analogy. Customers looking for any old tree will choose the one easiest to get—the cheapest one and the most convenient one. They will do that until someone else comes along and sells a cheaper and more convenient widget. I call this the "WalMart quotient."

If you want to compete at that level for market share, where your margins are shrinking and you're always losing to the newest big-box store with the deepest pockets, stop reading because this book is about building great, enduring companies based on value, not price. The kind of company that I celebrate and honor and believe will benefit you and your customers the most is one that doesn't worry about the next big-box store stealing market share, lowering everyone's margins and their happiness, and doing little to create a better place to work or to shop. Instead, this book urges companies to sell value, not price; provide solutions, not products; and to increase everyone's overall happiness and experiences.

And that brings me to your employees—the most important ingredients in your cake.

If you want a vanilla cake with no frosting and a sunken middle, hire hard-working people and think of ways to increase their productivity. I predict malaise, higher-than-necessary turnover rates, and a workforce devoid of new ideas. And the greatest crusher of all: employee word of mouth heavy enough to sink the brand that carries your products to market.

If you want a chocolate-chip cake made with the world's best chocolate and a creamy frosting that melts in your mouth, with a shape that lures you to heavenly places, hire hard-working people and think of ways to make them happy: Inspire them, motivate them, engage them, empower them, honor them, respect them, and reward them. You might need to provide additional tools and technology to increase their productivity, but you won't need to manage their productivity—they will strive to be the best they can be and to boost their own productivity levels to great heights. Your turnover rates will be lower than industry average, and employee word of mouth as well as employee interaction with customers and others outside the business will drive your Brand toward greatness.

Business leaders who understand human motivation and who want to do the right thing serve chocolate-chip cake. They lead with their hearts, they inspire passion for their business among employees and customers alike, and they work to add to the happiness of everyone they come in contact with.

These same leaders give back to their communities, as do their employees, and they allocate monies to improve the environment. Their reasons for doing these things might not be entirely altruistic, but they do know that doing good is good for business and profits, good for people (including themselves, their families, and their friends), and good for the planet.

Differentiation and Identification

If you identify the customers seeking your solutions and identify whatever it is that differentiates you from all your competitors (what makes you different from all the other widget makers), then you will be able to target your market based on the behaviors, emotions, demographics, psychographics, specific needs, and desires of those key customers. When you achieve this unique position, you gain a competitive edge and you stand a good chance of maximizing your profits.

Here is what I mean: If all I want is to make a cup of coffee at home at the best price, I am likely to purchase coffee in a can at a big-box store and an inexpensive coffee maker to brew it, or I would grab a cup from Duncan Donuts or from a fast-food restaurant.

But what if I have discriminating tastes and want only coffee made from the best Arabica beans? Will the canned coffee and the cheap coffeemaker or the restaurants provide a solution to meet my needs and wants?

Unlikely. I probably will choose the local café with high standards, or a coffee house run by a specialty coffee purveyor.

Local cafes and coffee companies that care about their customers' experiences with their products and services have identified their target markets and know how to reach them using targeted-market campaigns. More important, they understand their unique selling proposition, so they market to people who want the experience as well as a good cup of coffee.

Before you build your business plan, identify the ways you will separate yourself from your competitors. Unless you have lots of money to experiment with, I urge you to identify your differentiators and build your plan well before you open your business or launch a new product campaign. Then, identify your most profitable potential customers, and market to them using directed and targeted strategies. Employ such tactics as word of mouth, local advertising in carefully chosen media, direct mail, networking, and Web 2.0 tools (blogs, podcasts, etc.). Don't ignore reach, but don't bust your budget either, because this can lead to devastatingly short cash flows and perhaps even bankruptcy.

Here is how a typical business might address these concerns within its business plan:

> ### What does our business do?
>
> We help businesses that want to grow by focusing on sales and marketing processes, strategies and techniques, and leadership with a heart. A lot of companies focus on the wrong things and throw money at symptoms instead of solutions. We provide solutions for increasing sales. We guarantee it. We do this all within your budget, and we work closely with executives and managers to achieve success.
>
> ### What does our culture look like?
>
> We surround ourselves with partners who themselves are entrepreneurs. They lead with a heart, they are passionate about their Brand, they care more about their clients and customers than about their bottom lines, and they are motivated, honest, innovative, smart, and experienced. Their integrity is beyond reproach. And they create happiness.
>
> ### Who do we work with?
>
> Our clients are executives from companies located in the Northeast, including New England, New York, New Jersey, and Pennsylvania. Our clients are passionate, caring, imaginative, innovative, inspired, and inspirational. They are smart, motivated, and determined to grow. Our clients are action-oriented, committed to getting things done the right way, and open to change.

➲ Practical and Tactical Advice ⊂

Building the Business Plan

Business Plans do not come from a mold, but generally include the following components:

1. Title page
2. Table of contents
3. Executive summary
4. Business opportunity
5. Market
6. Competition
7. Management Team
8. Financials
9. Business risks
10. Exit strategy
11. Summary

Let's look at each section.

Title page. Take time to think about a good headline that employs nouns and verbs. Don't make the mistake of creating a business plan so drab that no one will ever read it. Remember that this is a working document. You are building a business with this plan, and if the plan is dull, the business will sound like a sleeper instead of an exciting enterprise that will sweep the market off its feet. Besides, the business plan should tell a story, and every good story starts with a good title. After the title, include the contact details—name, title, postal address, telephone number, and e-mail address.

Table of Contents. This may seem like a no-brainer, but every detail is important. The business plan is a short story, not a novel. Keep the plan to fewer than 40 pages if you want it read. The business plan makes up the foundation, walls, ceiling, and roof. The finer details — the interior designs — are spelled out in the strategic planning phase.

Executive Summary. This may be the most important section you write. Write it last, after the heavy lifting is done. Investors and executives initially spend only a few minutes looking at your plan. If you want the entire plan read, the summary must be compelling. Make sure the important information leaps out at the reader — use headlines, bullets, quotes, pictures, and testimonials. Write the summary in a way that grabs the reader's attention and makes the story about them. Tell them why they should care and inspire them to read on.

The Business Opportunity. What business opportunity does the investor care about? Summarize that opportunity in this section. If the business has a history, include it; if not, write a description of your products and services and why a market demand exists for those products and services. Explain what differentiates you from your competition. It is helpful to show why the management team has the competence to develop, deliver, service, market, and sell these products or services, especially if no business history exists.

Market. In this section, you must convince the reader that a market exists for your business's products and services. Describe that market in detail, including trends, size, and growth rate. Show what the market looks like. Convince the reader that you understand the market and its segments in great detail and that your business has a convincing strategy to conquer that market.

Competition. Here you describe the competition and explain your understanding of what they do and how and where they do it. It's also where you explain in detail your value proposition and your competitive positioning. What value do you offer the market that will lure customers to purchase your products and services over those of the competition? What are your strengths and your competitive advantages? How do you propose to maximize your strengths and maintain your competitive advantages? Discuss your weaknesses; honesty goes a long way toward creating credibility, and every business has weaknesses. Describing weaknesses as well as strengths suggests that you recognize both and can develop strategies to deal with or exploit them.

The Management Team. Employees, customers, and investors work, buy, and invest with people, not with a logo or an idea. Why should I trust the leadership of this business to succeed? Who are you? What relevant experiences do you bring to this business? What successes and failures lie in your past? (A famous software executive is often quoted as saying he likes to hire entrepreneurs who have failed, because they have it out of their systems and have learned from their mistakes.) Who are the key members of the team, and what do their business records look like? Include an organization chart, as well. What are the key functions of the business? What do the operations of the business look like? People like to know that careful thought has gone into the structure of the operations to ensure effectiveness and efficiency.

Financials. In this section, summarize the financial statement, business valuation, employee schedule, and supporting assumptions. Financial statements generally project over three to five years and contain best-, average-, and worst-case scenarios. If you are using the business plan to raise capital, be sure to show capital needed, the cash flow, and the net present value of the investment.

Business Risks. Every business faces risks—there are no sure things. Discuss the major risks here and the strategies you will launch and manage to minimize those risks.

Exit Strategy. How will you get out of this business in the future, if you want or need to?

Summary. Summarize the key points of each section. Remember: This is your last chance to make a great impression. In a piece of fiction, this is the denouement, the climax. But since it's a business plan, be sure you've restated your most important points in a compelling way.

Points to Ponder

- Create a business plan designed to bring people the happiness they deserve and want.

- Build it right the first time.

- Good planning followed by exceptional execution leads to more good than bad.

- Lead with your heart, and surround yourself with smart people who fit the kind of culture necessary for your success.

- Always think of people first.

- Develop authentic and heart-felt values, and filter every decision through your values.

- Always strive to create happiness.

- Write a business plan to sell the business concept to raise monies and to create a business built on a firm foundation.

- It is about building great, enduring companies based on value, not price.

- Inspire passion for your business among your employees and your customers.

- Give back to your community. It is good for business, good for profits, good for people (themselves, their families, and their friends), and good for the planet.

- Before you build your business plan, identify the ways you will separate yourself from your competitors.

Chapter Six
Strategic Plans That Work

This chapter lays out the basic premises behind one-and five-year strategic plans. Your strategic planning must reflect your values and be designed to positively affect people. Your goals should be measured not only in dollars and cents, but also by the positive impressions you leave on people. All of this can be measured qualitatively and quantitatively.

Strategy is more than a plan.

I was struck by what Don Peppers and Martha Rogers said in their article entitled *The Essence of Strategy*:

> "The word 'strategy' may be one of the most misused and misunderstood words in business today. Nine times out of 10, when you hear business executives talking about a strategy, what they are really talking about is simply a plan. But strategy implies so much more than planning. A well-played chess game involves strategy. A well-played solitaire game employs planning. A strategy should imply planning that is designed to out-maneuver a competitor or to defeat a rival's plan. It should include measures that will create a winning situation in a contest with opponents or in a struggle with forces working against the plan.

The military definition of strategy involves planning for success in a hostile environment, and we think this is probably the best and shortest definition of the word. A true business strategy, in other words, is a plan that anticipates the actions of your competitors or the resistance of others."

How can we lead with the heart when we think of strategy as out-maneuvering a competitor or defeating a rival's plan, or anticipating the actions or the resistance of others?

Leading with the heart and working to change a culture of greed where winners mean losers is not the same as leading with a bleeding heart. Business is about competition; it is about winning. It is about making difficult decisions that will negatively impact your competitors. It is about being confident and sometimes tough. You can be all those things and still lead with the heart, and still contribute to creating a culture of values where giving back for the greater good is more important than the size of your money tree or the number of competitors you defeated along the way.

Leading with the heart is not about eliminating competitors. You might weaken them and grab market share, and you should aim to do just that. Nevertheless, we need to approach competition as a good thing: It makes us better, stronger, and smarter. Without competition, mediocrity stands on our doorsteps waiting to turn us into Joe and Jane Average—not the kind of business people who will make a difference.

We want our competition to stay in the game, and we want them to lead with the heart, as well. If *they* don't run caring and concerned businesses and you do, your business will grab market share from them because of your business model and style. Greedy and uncaring business owners eventually eliminate themselves. They will shrivel and die or at the very least become irrelevant unless they change the way they conduct their business.

The petroleum industry is a great example of this. If these companies subscribed to the lead-with-the-heart business model, they would be pouring billions into R&D to eliminate our reliance upon fossil fuel. They would innovate and place themselves at the forefront of new technologies. Instead, they rush blindly into maximizing short-term profits and look to Alaska as a short-term solution for new product. Some oil companies claim to be innovating and developing new and cleaner technologies, but I don't see any great urgency on their part to invest the necessary monies to change our reliance on fossil fuels. It might not happen in my lifetime, but I am convinced that this industry's short-term thinking will lead to their ultimate demise, unless they move more quickly to invest in new sources of renewable and cheap energy.

The American automobile industry presents another example of a worn-out business model that is based on short-term profits and products no longer suited to the times. The Japanese had a vision three decades ago, and American manufacturers now rush to catch up. They are in a life-and-death struggle to survive because of their lack of will, courage, and vision, all forsaken because they chose short-term profits. They continue to produce cars that burn too much fuel and spew high levels of pollutants into the air.

The better you get at leading with the heart and the less able or willing your competition is to follow this business model, the more distance you will put between you and the pack, and the more passion and loyalty your Brand will engender. Your business margins will be greater, and your bottom line will be where it needs to be for you to be as big or as small as you want. What's more, your employees, your customers, and your communities will benefit from the way you practice business. Of this, I have no doubt.

We have good examples to follow, which to one degree or another align themselves with this prescription for success. Several have been mentioned in this book. They all fall somewhat short of the model presented here, but only because Wall Street causes companies to fret about and to focus too much energy and monies on strategies that create short-term profits. It's not because that fear is warranted, but rather because Wall Street understands little that can't be quantified immediately. Waiting for tomorrow is not an option.

When I was at Starbucks, I prepared several quarterly presentations for a conference call between Starbucks senior executives and the analysts who covered the industry. My inspiration came from men and women who led with the heart, were extraordinarily caring, and believed without a doubt that if they did the right thing for people, at the end of the day their numbers would compare favorably with or even exceed Wall Street's expectations. And they did and still do.

The day following the teleconference, analysts came out with their predictions. Although they were relatively optimistic, they were somewhat critical of the executive presentations because some focused on passion, caring, and treating people well. They were visionary, but they were not representative of the way most companies report progress and projections to Wall Street.

What companies like Starbucks have not yet done is to create momentum in the business world for others to follow their example. This may be partly because of humility or because company executives are themselves victims of a culture that believes we should measure success mostly by money. But if this world is to become a better place, companies such as Starbucks need to create this momentum.

The secret to shifting a culture is for smart leaders to digest varying points of view and put into action those that resonate within them the most. I don't expect established businesses, especially those with decades of baggage packed away within their corporate culture, to change much or to become leaders of a new movement. Nevertheless, I urge companies to continue to make improvements beneficial to the world. I look forward to the next generation of great businesses to test this model's premises with the faith and courage that it takes to succeed. Companies that have already begun to implement this model are succeeding and growing by leaps and bounds.

Where should you begin?

Begin the strategic planning process with competitive intelligence and market analysis. This way, you will understand and can take advantage of the similarities and differences between your business and others like it. More importantly, you will understand thoroughly what your clients and customers most want and need from the products and services that you offer.

Phase One

You need to learn why customers choose your competitors over you, and what barriers block your salespeople from success. This is what I refer to when I say strategic planning begins with competitive intelligence.

Competitive intelligence will tell you:

- How competitors position their products and services
- Their pricing strategies
- Their strengths
- Their weaknesses

From that research, you can then build a strategy to compete and succeed. Keep in mind that your customers define your competition. Be sure to ask for their opinions, as well as those of your salespeople. Of course, if they are smart, your rivals also apply competitive intelligence to their own strategic planning. Therefore, the strategies and the execution of your plan will determine who gains market share. On the other hand, if you don't apply competitive intelligence and your competitors do, you are in trouble.

Since a happy experience is what you strive most for and urge others to strive for as well, you must also do a market analysis. This increases your ability to create an experience that is not only wanted by your customers, but that also makes them feel like your services are designed just for them. When your customers experience your services in ways that make them feel as if they are your only customers, you succeed at achieving your mission.

You can create that special experience by finding out what kind of customer experience will build relationships with people. If your customers are other businesses, you also must make sure that your services are transferable in ways that meet your clients' needs and desired experiences.

Phase Two

Once you have collected and processed and digested all this competitive information, you need to narrow and then align your strategies throughout your entire business so that your plan focuses on grabbing greater market share while still retaining your current customer and client base.

The strategies must align with your business plan, as well—especially with your core purpose and your core values. You must focus entirely on building your Brand around these two things, and reject any and all business opportunities that are not already aligned with them.

Are strategic thinking and strategic planning really helpful?

A 1996 study by the Association of Management Consulting Firms found that executives, consultants, and business school professors generally agree that business strategy is the single most important management issue.[1] It still is, and should never be otherwise. The opposite of strategic planning is downsizing—a non-strategy that actually ends up hurting business growth and income in the long-term. Strong strategic planning, on the other hand, results in long-term gains and helps a business enterprise move along the upward curve, no matter the economy's ups and downs.

Strategic planning is different from what it was before the downsizing eras of the 1980s and 1990s, thanks to former General Electric chairman Jack Welch. Welch dismantled the company's planning department in 1983, where 200 senior-level staffers had been sweating over operating and financial details instead of focusing on competitive positioning.

In today's business environment, strategic planning is best accomplished through top-down and bottom-up planning and alignment. The company's executive team produces the overall strategic plan. Managers from all the functional areas then develop strategic plans to support and achieve the company's overall goals.

Jack Welch pushed responsibility for strategy down to each of General Electric's 12 unit heads, who met every summer with Welch and his top-management team for day-long planning sessions.

"The focus is on strategy, both near-term and a four-year look into the future," said Steven Kerr, GE's former vice president for corporate management development during those heady days when Welch reigned over the growing corporate giant. "They lay out what they are going to do, what new products they are interested in, and what their competition is doing."

Today there is no one at GE with the title of head of strategic planning. "If you had one, what would such a person do?" asks Kerr. "He would require reports." In other words, that position represents added and unnecessary bureaucracy.

A good plan does not guarantee success, however. Its execution must be carried out by capable managers who are held responsible and accountable for results and rewarded based on success. And because individuals are resistant to change, the company culture must be flexible, brand-savvy, and customer-centered. That means hiring the right people and getting rid of individuals who do not fit the culture best suited to your business.

If your initial business plan is built on values and happiness, your culture should be where it needs to be so that change will not be a huge problem for employees. When I read about company layoffs of thousands of workers, I immediately conclude that the company's executive team failed to grow appropriately and its workers are paying the price. Notice that stock prices often increase after big layoffs. What's wrong with that picture? It is just one more example of Wall Street's negative influence on business growth. The traders have overly influenced the company's executives to make bad short-term decisions.

Alignment is important. Every functional area, every person, and everything the business does must be aligned around the strategic plan's goals and objectives. Every person and every tactic must be targeted to achieve the company's primary goals. This step in the process can be challenging and time-consuming, but without it the plan is incomplete.

Ultimate responsibility lies with the company's leaders. They must measure and track how the company is performing against the goals. Executives and managers must not be allowed to set goals low just so they can easily achieve their bonuses. Again, you must put the right people in place: people who are willing to create, manage, and execute a strategic process designed to over-achieve for success.

Getting the Job Done

Here are the steps top management experts at the Wharton School recommend for developing a strategic plan that provides some incremental gains.

1. Develop a model for execution.
2. Choose the right metrics.
3. Work the plan.
4. Assess performance frequently.
5. Communicate

Don't blame the plan. Blame the boss!

Is there anyone in business foolish enough to assert that strategic planning is a waste of time? Well, yes, I suspect that at one point or another most of us decide that time spent on this endeavor is an exercise in futility.

Who, for example, has not spent month after month cooped up in meeting rooms, hammering out goals, strategies, tactics, and metrics for the purpose of measuring success, only to see the resulting plan filed on a shelf never to be seen again? Perhaps the result was instead utter frustration because you and your colleagues were trying to launch and manage a hard-won plan without true executive support at the start (but with plenty of criticism at the end for failing to make the numbers).

Management consulting firm Marakon Associates and the Economist Intelligence Unit surveyed senior executives at 197 companies in 2004. Only 63 percent of the respondents said they achieved the expected results of their strategic plans.

In a white paper entitled *Three Reasons Why Good Strategies Fail: Execution, Execution, Execution,* Wharton management professor Lawrence G. Hrebiniak stated that MBA-trained managers know a lot about how to develop a plan, but know very little about how to carry it out.

"Most of our MBAs receive great training in planning but far less in execution," explained Hrebiniak. "Even though they are good managers, over time they really have to learn through the school of hard knocks, through experience, which means they make a lot of mistakes."

My 35 years of experience in the corporate world and as an entrepreneur tells me that the Marakon results and Hrebiniak's comments are on target. Managers tend to be enthusiastic about their strategic planning, but get disheartened when executives fail to execute the promise of innovation and reinvention held within those pages.

Analysis of why some leaders fail to execute their strategic plan suggests that shareholders and board members are part of the problem. As long as they insist upon short-term results, only the most powerful and fearless executives will reap the long-term rewards and margins that strategic planning can deliver. Meanwhile, short-term thinking prevents American businesses, small and large alike, from becoming the best they can be. In the long-term, this short-term thinking shortchanges everyone, including shareholders.

Need proof? In April 2007, *Consumer Reports* came out with their annual list of the most-reliable cars. "The Japanese and South Koreans continue to make the most reliable vehicles, with 11 problems per 100 vehicles on average. U.S. automakers follow, with 16 problems per 100. European manufacturers continue to lag, with 19 problems per 100." the accompanying article stated. I do not believe for a moment that American engineers and workers are any less competent than their Japanese counterparts. That leaves leadership, innovation, and planning as the culprits behind the failure of the American automotive industry. If Ford and GM continue to miscalculate their customers' needs, wants, and desires and continue to fail to look toward society's future needs, they will go out of business or be taken over by a foreign company.

Fortunately, America is still blessed with brave and bold business leaders attempting to pilot American businesses toward greatness. As James C. Collins and Jerry I. Porras put it, "Maximizing shareholder wealth or profit maximization has not been the dominant driving force or primary objective through the history of the visionary companies." Ironically, they say, such visionary companies do achieve long-term financial returns, and manage to become part of the very fabric of society.

If you plan accordingly, set big goals, hire the right people, and build a culture of success, you too can drive your Brand to magnificent results. If you also encourage personal responsibility and calculated risk-taking, practice integrity in everything you do, employ cross-functional best practices, encourage and experiment with creativity and innovation, and strive for happiness, how can you not be among the best at what you do?

Know your workers' needs as well as your customers' needs.

A strategic plan must take into consideration the company's employees, if it is to succeed. Executives need to understand workers' needs and challenges, and create plans that those workers can focus on and contribute to.

One of today's greatest challenges for workers is productivity. Technology might be the primary culprit when it comes to declining productivity. In today's workplaces, workers say they are rushed and are getting less done than they did some 10 years ago.

"Technology has sped everything up and, by speeding everything up, it's slowed everything down, paradoxically," said John Challenger, chief executive of Chicago-based outplacement consultants Challenger, Gray and Christmas. "We never concentrate on one task anymore. You take a little chip out of it, and then you're on to the next thing. It's harder to feel like you're accomplishing something."

Sixty percent of workers say they always or frequently feel rushed, Wulforst reports. Those who say they feel extremely productive or very productive dropped to 51 percent.

In 2006, American workers showed increases in productivity, although technology advances continue to pressure workers to do more. Whether or not technology improves or decreases productivity, happier, passionate, and engaged employees will be more productive than others. Executives need to create a work environment that regularly trains workers to deal with new technology and the stress that comes with using it.

Companies need to be flexible with workers' time and make sure workers have control over their tasks. Workers who have flexible hours and feel in control are more productive. Bosses who micro-manage, on the other hand, make the problem worse. Downsizing leaves fewer workers doing the work, dramatically increasing stress.

Technology is but one more reason business leaders need to understand their employees' wants, needs, and desires. If employees don't have the time to complete a task before moving on to the next one, how can any plan succeed? You must first fix the time problem before you create a plan that adds additional work to an employee's schedule.

Be bold—innovate.

"If you don't like change, you're going to like irrelevance even less."
> — General Eric Shinseki
> Chief of Staff, U.S. Army

"A focus on cost-cutting and efficiency has helped many companies weather the downturn, but this approach will ultimately render them obsolete. Only the constant pursuit of innovation can ensure long-term success."
> — Daniel Muzyka
> Dean of Sauder School of Business,
> University of British Columbia

"It is not the strongest of the species that survives, or the most intelligent, but the one most responsive to change."
> —Charles Darwin

Innovation has become a buzzword and a cliché, and that worries me. *You must be innovative* and you must reinvent yourself regularly if you are to address the ever-changing conditions that affect your business.

In the past, some businesses mistook diversity of products and services for innovation. They went outside their core businesses and what they do best, which drained their profits to such an extent that some of them never recovered.

Jeffrey R. Immelt, GE's Chairman and CEO, says that his company's new imperatives are risk-taking, sophisticated marketing, and innovation." Strong, successful businesses do the following:

---

1. Smart and appropriate cost-cutting

2. Efficiencies at every level

3. Win-win deals

4. Continuous improvement throughout the business

5. Calculated risk taking

6. Killer marketing

7. Innovation that stays ahead of the curve when possible

8. A culture that always reacts rapidly to change

IBM recently surveyed 750 CEOs, and found that the best sources of innovative ideas are employees (41 percent), business partners (38 percent), customers (36 percent), and R&D (14 percent).

One of the global study's key findings, according to Marc Chapman, IBM global leader of strategy and change services, is that executives are focusing on innovation and are looking outside the company for new ideas.

People who know about corporate R&D will tell you that few companies do it better than Procter & Gamble. When the company grew into a $70 billion business, it changed its strategy to "connect and develop." Technology and networks are being mined for new ideas on future products, because the old "do-it-yourself" model is no longer able to produce 4–6 percent annual growth. P&G now acquires at least 50 percent of its innovations externally. Half of the company's innovations come from inside the company and half come from scientists and engineers who don't work for P&G. This helps make sure the company clearly understands consumer needs.

The number-one concern of CEOs is steady top-line growth. Innovation looks more and more like the key to that growth.

Buying or Working Your Way to Growth

"Not a single company that qualified as having made a sustained transformation ignited its leap with a big acquisition or merger. Moreover, comparison companies—those that failed to make a leap or, if they did, failed to sustain it—often tried to make themselves great with a big acquisition or merger. They failed to grasp the simple truth that while you can buy your way to growth, you cannot buy your way to greatness."

—Jim Collins

Banking and insurance industries far too often use mergers and acquisitions as growth tools. I discourage my clients from taking this approach. You grow by being customer-centered and innovative and by creating great experiences. It is not about being bigger. It is about being better.

Separate yourself from the pack.

Staying within this theme, how do you differentiate your company from all other businesses with similar products and services? How do you innovate?

Here are two real-life examples of innovative marketing attitudes:

- Progressive does not sell insurance. It sells speed of service.

- Harley Davidson does not sell motorcycles. It sells image in the form of a 40-something accountant riding through town and having people terrified of him.

    Consider these observations:

    "Ninety percent of what you call management consists of making it difficult for people to get things done."
    — Peter Drucker

"You have a strategic plan. It's called doing things."
    — Herb Kelleher, CEO of
    Southwest Airlines

"People want to be part of something larger than themselves. They want to be part of something they're really proud of, that they fight for, sacrifice for, and trust."

— Howard Schultz

As you begin the process of reinventing (or inventing) your business, bear this in mind:

"The greatest danger for most of us is not that our aim is too high and we miss it, but that it is too low and we reach it."

—Michaelangelo

➔ Practical and Tactical Advice ◖

For those brave and bold enough to want to join the ranks of the visionaries, consider these suggestions to help your strategic planning and its execution:

1. Do annual strategic plans. Tie them to your overall business plan, and measure progress quarterly. This applies to all businesses, whether you run a sole proprietorship or a mega multinational corporation.

2. Think long-term. Be flexible and be resilient so that you can change course quickly to keep from going over the falls.

3. Set high goals, short-term and long-term. Don't be intimidated by Wall Street or the boardroom. Those who merely set goals they can easily make in order to impress investors only slowly get around to stretching their business to achieve greatness, if ever.

4. Use metrics to measure every goal in every functional area. Don't let anyone escape by saying that they really can't measure what they do. If they can't figure out a way to measure what they do, get rid of them. They are not a good fit for this business model.

5. Align every department and every employee so that every ounce of the business's energy is directed at achieving the goals set within the business plan and then in this year's strategic plan. There should be no individual or departmental goals that fail to support the overall business goals. Break down silos so that every hand is tightly holding every other hand.

6. Evaluate every department and every employee on how they contribute to achieving the goals. Tie their pay, bonuses, and benefits directly to success or failure.

7. Make the focus of the plan marketing and sales. Every person in every business should understand the goals of marketing and sales, and work daily to achieve them.

8. Communicate, communicate, and communicate! If you want your plan to succeed, every member of your culture must be engaged and informed.

These recommendations make up only a few slices of the puzzle, yet they represent solid principles that drive business planning. Remember this: A plan is only as good as the leader or boss driving it and the people executing it.

Points to Ponder

• As in all you do within your business, your strategic planning is filtered through your values.

• Your goals are measured not only in dollars and cents, but also by the positive impressions you leave on people. All these things can be measured qualitatively and quantitatively.

• Business is about competition. It is about winning. It is about making difficult decisions that may negatively impact your competitors. It is about being confident and sometimes tough. You can be all those things and still lead with the heart and contribute to creating a culture of values.

• Giving back for the greater good should be more important than measuring winning by the size of your money tree or the number of competitors you defeated along the way.

• Competition is good, because it makes us better and smarter.

• Greedy and uncaring business owners eventually eliminate themselves. Unless they change the ways they conduct their businesses, they will shrivel and possibly die.

• If you lead with the heart, you will separate yourself from the pack, and your Brand will engender passion and loyalty.

Chapter Seven
Building the Strategic Plan

Strategic planning begins with the business plan, which is the foundation of your business. You can adjust your business plans to reflect changes within your business model, goal, or rate of success, but you must have one. Without a business plan, it will be difficult to develop a strategic plan that maximizes your business's potential. It would be like building a house atop a sand dune without first setting down a proper foundation.

Why? Because a business plan sets forth who and what you are, where you want to go, and how you will get there. It is long-term. A strategic plan is short-term. It should be an annual creation that is flexible, measurable, and easily revised if necessary. Some companies develop five-year strategic plans to accompany their one-year plan. I consider this to be short-term planning, as well.

The company's official Strategic Plan spells out how to achieve annual milestones that will build the value promised within its official Business Plan. Each functional area within the company needs to create its own strategic plan after the organization's plan is created—a plan that does no more or no less than what is needed to support and achieve the organization's strategic goals and objectives. Functional-area plans describe how each department or functional area will contribute to the company's Strategic Plan. Without that alignment and common focus, the business ends up with lots of platoons marching to their own beat, slowly getting picked off by the competition's army, which marches in lockstep.

The greatest challenges to creating a strategic plan are alignment and a common focus. Before writing the plan, leaders must ask and answer these two questions: 1) What determines which ideas are funded? And 2) How can I shape, manage, and give direction to the process? These two questions usually create the most dissent within the planning process, and can lead to disastrous results if handled improperly.

If you don't have complete agreement among managers and a resource allocation process that everyone participated in and understood, the strategic plan that emerges in practice will likely be different from the one on paper. Get your functional areas out of their individual silos and aligned with the company. This promotes buy-in, increases productivity, allocates resources as needed, and moves the business as one unit running together toward the finish line to win the race, outmaneuvering even the best of the competition's plans and structures (or, at the worst, staying even).

Present State

Begin developing a strategic plan by first getting executives to agree on and write down the present state of your company. Do due diligence—know and understand what the various approaches do and how to implement them. If you want an outside perspective, hire a consultant who can meet your needs. Often, consultants can more easily define your present state, because they are not worried or defensive about how their department's performance contributed to the company's current state. They are under no pressure to defend what worked and what didn't work last year.

Whether or not you bring in outside help, here are the questions that need to be answered:

- Where are you today?

- Are you on track, and hitting your milestones?

- Are you achieving your goals and your margins?

- What is working? Why?

- What is not working? Why not?

- Is your culture running smoothly? Or is it in need of a tune-up?

- Do you have the right people in the right positions?

- What is the competition doing? (Competitive and/or market research analysis must be completed before the strategic plan can be developed.)

- What do customers think about you?

- How does the world you operate in perceive your Brand?

Those are some of the questions that need to be addressed from a variety of points of view. The team that should answer those questions needs to be made up of the chief executive officer, the chief financial officer, the chief operations officer, and every department or functional area head. By diversifying the team, you make sure that you get various points of view, which increases your chances of being thorough.

The Future State: Where do you want to go?

Now that you know where you are, where do you need to go over the next year? What are your goals? Define your destination precisely in order to create meaningful goals. This "future state" analysis grows out of the research and analysis you did during the "present state" phase, as well as your growth and profit needs based on your Business Plan and such external factors as the current state of the economy. Use measurable destination points or milestones so that you can evaluate how you are doing as you travel toward your destination.

Gap Analysis

Once you know where you are and where you need to go, you must perform a gap analysis to determine exactly what needs to be done to get where you want to be over the next year.

By the way, if you are behind in achieving your previous milestones or you need to revise them because you realize that they won't ultimately lead you to success, the analysis should shine a light on the path to show you where you need to go and what you need to do to get back on track.

Your Strategic Plan should be updated every year. Think of it as an extension of the previous year's Strategic Plan that makes up for any shortfalls and reflects superior results from the previous year's goals.

For example, if you exceeded your goals last year and are ahead of schedule, you might be full of yourself and consequently set goals that are too low. This is not the time to breathe easy. See it as a great new opportunity to take advantage of your solid performance by stretching the goals more than ever before. Don't rest on yesterday's laurels; you'll be making a disastrous mistake.

Creating Goals

Goals should make you stretch, but they should also be achievable, realistic, and measurable. They are stepping stones for next year's Strategic Plan. They should not be set so that executives will be able to earn bonuses. If they are, then you have two problems: an inappropriate executive compensation package, and poor executive performance.

Keep the goals to no more than three, which provides more than enough challenge. Remember that there will be more than three goals overall, as each functional area needs to develop its own three goals to support and achieve the business's goals. If you have four departments, you will be driving and managing 15 goals—three overall goals, and 12 department goals supporting the overall goals.

Make the goals specific to your company's needs and designed to get you where you want to go. (And do not let anyone in a functional area say they are unable to create measurable goals. That is a tired and false response.) Here are some examples of specific goals:

- We will increase margins by xx percent.
- We will increase market share by xx percent.
- We will increase productivity by xx percent.

Calculated Risk Taking

Great and visionary companies go beyond setting goals that are easy to achieve, and they do not worry about the unexpected turns. Great leaders are visionary, and take calculated risks. They aren't afraid to try different things to see what works. Doing the same things over and over again because *That is the way we do things around here,* is not innovative or visionary, and it is bad for business.

Normally, it's not a good idea to change strategies in mid-stream. If it is necessary, add to them or change a few tactics to achieve them. Sometimes the best strategies are those that involve risk and never-before-tried thinking that will take several years to prove themselves. They are not necessarily going to be in our best-practices folders, but they might end up there some day.

Leaders should take calculated risks, but they also should encourage employees at every level to do the same. It works! For example, a 3M employee years ago overheard a customer who owned an auto paint shop complain about not being able to find a good adhesive tape. The employee, Dick Drew, returned to 3M and invented a masking tape. Drew went on to invent Scotch Tape. Both of those products made it onto the market because 3M listens to employees and encourages original thinking.

3M also encourages its people to pursue their ideas. It hires good workers and then leaves them alone to do their jobs. The company encourages experimentation and exudes this encouragement. It wants its people to give things a try.

Here's another example of what encouragement does: An employee at a Starbucks store in southern California noticed that a nearby competitor's store was selling a blended iced coffee drink with great success. The Starbucks employee created a recipe, and the store had a new blended drink. Starbucks improved on the original recipe, and the Frappuccino was born.

Encouraging employee-calculated risk-taking and innovation makes people happier and more productive, not to mention better able to contribute to the bottom line.

If you hire the right executives, your business — no matter its size — can be inventive and innovative with ever-increasing levels of happiness for all. Entrepreneurial start-ups and small companies tend to think more outside-the-box than do big corporations. The point of this section is that while strategic planning is necessary, it does not take the place of risk taking and the inventive spirit, no matter the size of the company or its cash flow. At the end of the day, it isn't about the plan; it's about action and the results from that action.

The Strategies to Achieve the Goals

A Strategic Plan should only be used for the upcoming fiscal or calendar year. You must review, analyze, and adjust your plan quarterly.

"Strategic planning used to mean a fairly rigid commitment for a set number of years. But try locking in a long-term plan today, and the world will pass you by. The turbulent business environment demands that corporate leaders make frequent strategic adjustments. Companies must be prepared to abandon their current course and launch off on a different path every time the market shifts or a new opportunity emerges," writes Tad Leahy in a 2003 article in Business Finance.

"Strategic flexibility sounds like an oxymoron," says Michael E. Raynor of Deloitte Consulting in Toronto in that same article. "Strategy is about commitment to market positions, technologies, and customers. Flexibility is about avoiding commitment, about creating the ability to bob and weave, to exploit whatever opportunities come along. Strategic flexibility is a way to combine the power of commitment-based strategy with the benefits of flexibility in the face of an unpredictable environment."

The lead-with-the-heart approach takes the best from a variety of concepts, and melds them. It encourages flexibility and commitment.

➲ Practical and Tactical Advice ➲

Options
Creating strategies is about looking at all your options and then making hard choices about the two or three goals you plan to focus on over the next year. Thoroughly analyze and address these options before you identify the

goals. Then direct your strategies toward achieving the goals. Ask questions like these when choosing options:

Customers

- What do most customers want from us and from our competitors? What do they get?
- What will our customers most want from us and from our competitors in one year, five years, and ten years? What will they get?
- What are our customers' biggest needs, wants, and desires?
- Do we meet their needs, wants, and desires? How well do we meet them?
- What do we need to do to put every customer need together with the right solution?

Competitors

- How are our competitors meeting customer needs differently and/or better?
- What unique solutions do our competitors provide?
- What are our competitors planning to launch in the next year? The next five years? The next 10 years? How should we respond?

Internal Factors

- What does our performance look like? How does it affect the Strategic Plan?
- Are we aligned?
- Does every employee know, understand, and work toward the goals?
- Do our compensation packages reflect the degree to which we achieve our goals?

- What do we do best? How do we exploit those things to increase our profits?
- Where are we losing money? How do we stop doing those things?
- What are our strengths and our weaknesses? How do we become stronger? How do we fix the areas where we are weak?
- What are our barriers to success?
- How much can we budget to achieve the Strategic Plan?

External Factors
- What is happening in the environment that will impact the Plan? In the economy? In our customers' lives? In technology? In the regulatory environment?

The Strategies

Your list of factors and questions will vary according to your business. The key to creating goals and strategies is to address every factor that will affect your bottom line in the coming year by asking such questions, and carefully reviewing the answers. Then create goals and strategies to increase your competitive abilities and your profits. Finally, make certain that your budget and available staff are enough to do everything that is called for in your plan.

For example, let's assume you are losing market share to a competitor and it is seriously impacting your bottom line to the extent that if you cannot grow out of this problem, you will need to cut costs. Your goal and the strategies to achieve that goal might look like this:

- **Goal:** To increase the bottom line by 15 percent by grabbing 10 percent market share from XYZ Company; by increasing margins by 3 percent; and by increasing customer retention by 15 percent. (Average customer defection in early 2007 stood at about 25 percent.)

- **Strategy:** To analyze the cause for the loss of market share to XYZ Company by March.

- **Strategy:** To aggressively regain market share with a plan directed at closing the gap between our company and XYZ Company by December.

- **Strategy:** To aggressively address our customer wants, needs, and desires; to address our management program; and to increase retention rates.

The Tactics to Achieve the Strategies

Tactics revolve around the tools and methods you use to achieve the strategies. They should be detailed, quick to launch, easily managed, and well within the budget set asides. Most importantly, the tactics, like everything you do in business, should be integrated. Each one should support each other one, often in a linear manner.

You might use competitive intelligence to develop tactics for these sample strategies:

Tactic One: Competitive Intelligence

The approach described in this section comes from Fred Wergeles and Associates, providers of competitive intelligence.[1]

Competitive Intelligence refers to the information gathered through the use of proven and legal collection and analysis techniques for a variety of business functions, including strategic planning, mergers, acquisitions and alliances, marketing and sales, and product development. This helps a company to answer such questions as:

- Who is winning in your market? Why?

- Should you protect against a particular competitor's strengths?

- Should you take advantage of a competitor's weaknesses?

- Will your strategy transform the nature of competition?

- Do the ways in which your competitors are trying to compete suggest an even better alternative for you?

- What might your competitors do next?

- How are your customers' needs changing? How can you best satisfy them?

Corporate executives use competitive intelligence to develop their strategic plans, identify opportunities, and provide early warning of competitive threats. It allows them to challenge their underlying market assumptions, so they can plan for and even rehearse a myriad of future market scenarios. Such information can help answer the critical question *What if . . .?* The future-oriented perspective of competitive analysis enables executives to evaluate their current and future investments, manage risks, provide new ideas on business operations, and improve their reaction time to industry developments.

When properly done, a competitive intelligence system can deliver significant benefits to an organization. These benefits fall into four categories:

- Early warning

- Greater understanding of competitors' capabilities and intention (to "out-think" them and learn from their successes)

- More-informed decision making (strategically and operationally)

- Enhanced strategic planning and strategy formulation (derived from a greater understanding of the company's competitive environment and business future)

By developing an effective competitive intelligence system, a company also can enhance the performance of its sales and marketing teams by providing important information about customers, suppliers, and competitors, as well as by sharing critical market information. Competitive intelligence enables companies to exploit opportunities more quickly than their competitors and avoid potential threats.

Tactic Two: Market Research

Market research is often more about consumer research than competitor research. It can focus on competitors, but it is best used to focus on understanding the psychological and behavioral actions of consumers.

Your goal in employing market research is to understand why some customers buy from you and some don't, and to identify their needs, wants, and desires.

To get this information, these tools can be useful:

- **Test marketing:** A small-scale product or service launch to determine the potential of your product or service to capture a broader market.

- **Concept testing:** Used to discover whether or not potential customers and clients will find the product or service useful.

- **Mystery shopping:** Used to determine whether or not your stores, Web sites, and other outlets meet the customer service standards expected, and that your products and services are easily purchased.

- **Demand estimation:** Used to determine the demand for products or services.

- **Sales forecasting:** Used to determine the expected level of sales.

- **Customer satisfaction studies:** Used to determine customer satisfaction levels and the quality of the transaction.

- **Segmentation research:** Used to determine demographic, psychographic and behavioral characteristics of potential buyers.

- **Consumer decision-process research:** Used to determine what motivates people to buy, and to identify their decision-making processes.

- **Positioning research:** Used to determine how the market views your brand, compared to your competitors' brands.

There are other market research tools you can use, but these represent a good sampling of what you will need.

There are two methods you should consider using for market research:

1. Qualitative marketing research, such as focus groups, interviews, and projective techniques

2. Quantitative marketing research, such as surveys and questionnaires

When you outsource or hire market researchers, do your homework. Ask these questions first:

- What is the market research company's experience and background?

- Does this company believe in customizing to meet your needs, or do they sell a standard process?

- How well does this company work within its client's culture? Are they flexible within a team environment?

- When you interview prospective market-research consultants, do they ask lots of questions, listen well, and come back to you with a plan of attack that makes sense and stays within your budget?

- Are the prospective market researchers willing to employ creative techniques, as well as experimentation?

You will not always need market research *and* competitive intelligence, but there will be times when both are called for.

Tactic Three: The Plan of Attack

With your research and analysis in hand, you are ready to launch, manage, and execute the tactics to aggressively regain share. You have a plan directed at closing the perceived customer gap between your company and XYZ Company.

Keep in mind that we are talking about an overall strategic plan. These goals, strategies, and tactics form the foundation on which departmental strategic plans can be built.

For example, sales and marketing will play a huge role in achieving this goal, but it will be the responsibility of the sales and marketing functional area or the outsourced sales and marketing consulting firm to create the detailed plan to achieve this goal and these strategies.

In this sample plan, you list the tactics certain functional areas will take on, as well as the details. Competitive intelligence and marketing research, for example, might be handled by the marketing functional area, or outsourced and overseen by the appropriate in-house manager or executive. (Note: When work is outsourced, you must assign an in-house manager to oversee that work. Leaving it to the consultant is a bad idea and is not in their or your best interests.)

If you do not have an internal department to do the work but you will not be outsourcing it, you will end up taking on the roles and creating each necessary detailed plan to achieve the goals. That is a mistake! Either create the departments internally with the best people you can hire, or put consulting in your budgets.

In addition to competitive intelligence and market research, you might add tactics that include such things as public relations; advertising; enhanced customer service; customer relationship management; improved supply chain; enhanced products and services at the same price; special introductory offers; innovative customer management; and media that allow you to talk with your customers and them to talk back to you.

Aligning Every Part of the Business

Alignment is a very important key issue. It also is the most difficult task to achieve. With alignment,

- Every piece of the business is operating from one overall Strategic Plan.

- Every department or functional area creates a plan committed to supporting and achieving the company's Strategic Plan.

- Every piece of the business is evaluated each quarter for progress.

- Monies are provided to achieve success.

- Each piece of the business and every person in the business is rewarded based on their contribution to achieving the annual Strategic Plan.

Without alignment, you will get the same results a NASCAR team gets when one of its members fails to execute: The car loses time or crashes into the wall. In either case, it loses.

The Metrics to Measure Success

Metrics can come in a variety of forms. Revenues and margins are easy to measure. Other goals and strategies may require market research through the use of surveys and focus groups. By the way, do not ignore anecdotal evidence: Customers and employees should be brought into the loop at every level of decision making to share their thoughts and feedback on your plan. In fact, the best customer research is when a business talks to them where they are, listens, and then adjusts its services based on what they learn. Blogging and other communication tools can be used for this also. Get employees and managers out of the office and into the places where your customers play, work, and shop so they know what people want.

The key is to measure correctly, precisely, and quarterly, and to use that data to revise the tactics to achieve the strategies you propose. At a minimum, you need to ask and answer the following questions: How many things should you measure? What metrics are important? Should you trust the numbers?

And, of course, once those questions are asked and answered, you need to ask *What should I do next?*

It is usually costly and inefficient to change strategies in midstream. When you measure the next quarterly results, you might find yourself back to square one. If you do not get the strategies correct from the beginning, something is wrong with the process. Executives and managers should be able to identify which strategies are needed to achieve the stated goals.

We all know how hard it is to measure success. I've worked in several corporate departments that handled internal and external relations and communications. I was often tempted to whine "*You just can't measure that!*", but I knew I would have to commit to measuring all that I did. Everything in a business environment is measurable.

Let's take public relations as an example. I don't care how many papers publish a particular press release. What I want to know is how many of the papers that reach my target audiences publish the release! And I want to know the level of impact on our target audiences. Is your press release working to achieve your goals? To do so, you need to use such tools as focus groups and surveys made up of people who subscribe to the newspapers that will publish your press releases, and then find out what, if anything, they get from the release. You also can use employee subscribers. This is a useful and less expensive strategy, but the results might be different and less valuable because employees have inside knowledge that will color their perceptions of the newspaper article.

You must measure everything you do if you are to maximize success. In fact, if a functional area's goals cannot be measured, shut it down or get a new department head who understands how to establish and measure goals. And make sure you measure for results, not for intangibles. This might sound heartless, but an employee who cannot achieve his or her goals should find work elsewhere. You do them no good by accepting their failures. Sometimes you can train them to overcome their weaknesses, but you must decide whether or not that is worth trying.

Budgeting for Success

The two most important factors in business success are happiness (creating and immersing everything you do in happiness) and alignment. If planning and budgeting are not completely aligned, I suspect you will not maximize your potential, no matter the happiness or anything else you add to your business, because your strategic and business plans cannot succeed if you fail to execute properly—delivering happiness and executing every element within this business model. Think of your business as an engine of commerce with one of your wheels out of alignment. You will never achieve maximum and steady performance until you align those wheels.

Far too often, budgets are fixed in their departmental silos, out of alignment with the company's goals and objectives. A department might achieve its stated goals, yet do little or nothing to contribute to the business's overall success. No monies should be budgeted for anything unless and until Business Plan and Strategic Plan budgets are aligned and approved with and by the finance department, the executive team, or the business owner (or whomever holds the purse strings). Only then should the company and department budgets include and evaluate all the other items within the budget that are necessary to run a cost-effective yet great business.

How might this work? Do the following:

1. Understand the company's current state.

2. Determine where you need to go.

3. Analyze your financials in detail.

4. Determine what needs to be done to grow your business.

5. Develop a strategic plan to achieve success in which every goal, strategy, and tactic is measurable.

6. Create a budget.

7. And then, hold everyone in the company accountable for achieving the goals.

Tying Performance Appraisals and Compensation to Success

Cross the finish line together or you don't cross it at all is common advice in sports and in business. You cross the finish line when you

1. Create plans.

2. Set goals and objectives.

3. Measure everything.

4. Align and allocate your resources to achieve planning goals and objectives.

5. Create a culture within which everyone is held accountable for achieving the goals and objectives.

6. Tie everyone's pay to their level of success in achieving the goals and objectives, with no exception.

When this is done, you create a road map that is understood and followed by the entire team. You achieve buy-in from everyone (and help those who cannot buy in find work elsewhere). When you are all on the same page, productivity increases, performance increases, and costs decrease, and employees and customers are happier, more satisfied, and more productive. Customers will buy more from your company.

Leadership by Example

Nothing discussed in this book happens unless leadership leads, which is very different from a leadership team that manages. Managing is yesterday's news. Great companies and those that want to be great will hire executives, directors, and middle managers who know the difference between leading and managing, and who themselves are leaders.

Leaders show, they don't tell. They lead by example. They clearly communicate their expectations, and their expectations are always at the highest levels. They represent the values of the company, and they hire for those values. They give their staffs all the tools necessary to be successful, including training and regular feedback, and then they get out of the way. Their door is always open, and they maintain the highest levels of integrity and expect their staffs to do so, as well. They demand respect and dignity throughout their areas of responsibility, and they are always respectful and dignified. They expect success and accept nothing less.

Research from The Forum Corporation tells us that leaders have some things in common.

Signs of Good Leadership

A strong intellect: Able to grasp new ideas quickly, engage in complex thinking, and be comfortable with ambiguity.

Technical capability: Possesses in-depth knowledge of the organization's industry, business models, and operations.

Emotional intelligence: Strong, self-aware, self-controlled, and able to develop and maintain strong relationships.

Adaptive capacity: Learns from experience, listens and responds to feedback, and adjusts quickly to new situations.

A track record of success: Accomplished at combining all of these capabilities to get work done effectively with and through others in order to drive business results.

In 2004, Marakon Associates surveyed senior executives from 197 large companies worldwide to determine how successful companies translate strategies into performance.

The study, published in 2005, found that senior executives struggle to achieve their long-range plans, but the processes they use to develop plans and measure results don't tell them if the failure to achieve the goals stems from poor planning, poor execution, both, or neither.

The survey also found that companies rarely track performance of their long-term plans; long-term results rarely meet projections; the gaps between strategies and results are substantial, and management often fails to recognize performance problems. Under-performance creates an under-performing culture, the study concluded.

Companies that follow many of the same strategies inherent in the lead-with-your-heart business model avoid these difficulties. They set realistic goals and objectives, they align their strategies and their staffs to achieve those goals and objectives, they measure performance frequently to judge how they are performing, and they allocate the appropriate resources to succeed.

Leaders motivate, inspire, and get things done. Without leadership, any strategic plan will fail, as will the business.

Points to Ponder

- Your Business Plan remains forever the foundation of your business.

- The Business Plan sets forth who and what you are, where you want to go, and how you will get there. It is long-term.

- The Strategic Plan should be an annual creation that is flexible, measurable, and easily revised. It is short-term.

- The Strategic Plan tells us how to achieve annual milestones that will build the value promised within the Business Plan.

- Develop a company Strategic Plan. Each functional area must then create a plan that does no more or no less than outline what is needed to support and achieve the organization's strategic goals and objectives.

- Functional area plans describe how each department (functional area) will contribute to the company's Strategic Plan.

- While companies might have an intended strategy, the strategy that actually emerges can be very different.

(continued)

Points to Ponder *(concluded)*

- Unless you achieve complete alignment, the strategic plan that emerges likely will be different from the one on paper.

- To build your strategic plan, start by evaluating your business's present state.

- Now that you know where you are, where do you need to go over the next year? This is the part of the plan that leads you to your goals.

- When you know where you are and where you need to go, you must perform a gap analysis to determine how much needs to be done to get where you need to be.

- The goals should make you stretch, but they should also be achievable and realistic.

- The goals should be stepping stones for next year's Strategic Plan.

- The goals need to be measurable.

- Great leaders are visionary, and they take calculated risk.

- Strategic flexibility is a must.

- Great companies and those that want to be great will hire executives, directors, and middle managers who know the difference between leading and managing, and who themselves are leaders.

Chapter Eight
Sales and Marketing That Work

Here is the truth most of us don't want to hear: Without marketing and sales, there is no business. Performing marketing and sales tasks is scary. We have to communicate with other people if we want to market the business and sell our products and services. Sometimes we do it by telephone (telemarketing). Sometimes we do it using mail (direct mail). Sometimes we use newspapers and magazines to tell our story (public relations). Sometimes we buy space in publications or online (advertising). And sometimes we use online tools such as Web sites, blogs, podcasts.

Marketing gets the word out about our business. It gets us noticed. It gets customers through our doors. It is the step that leads to sales, when a customer buys our products and services. If we don't get noticed and sell our products and services, there is no business.

Those who work in sales and marketing with complete honesty and integrity strive to increase happiness by making sure that the business creates products and delivers services that meet people's needs. Everyone involved in the business should treat all people with respect and dignity and talk with their current and potential customers, not at them. Communication is black or white and honest, or it is dishonest. When done correctly, sales and marketing tasks educate, inform, and reach out to specific people (our market) with news and information that people need to know about your business. And information that they can use to meet their wants, needs, and desires.

Here is the bottom line: Sales and marketing professionals care about people and their needs and share the information the public needs to make good choices in their lives. This is what we define as leading with the heart and creating happiness.

Think about it: If we are to manage a business for success, we have to create a business built around sales, marketing, and innovation because these are the most fundamental and most important tasks in an enterprise. Every person in the company has some responsibility for sales and marketing results, and their pay should be tied to those results. It doesn't matter whether or not the employee is in the accounting department or the marketing department: Every time an employee communicates with a customer, he or she is performing a marketing and a sales task.

The CSO Insights Sales Performance Optimization 2007 Survey Results and Analysis provides data that tells us the business community as a whole is not doing great work in sales and marketing:

- Only 60% of sales reps are making or exceeding quotas.

- Only 37% of firms report that they have implemented a formal sales process.

- 85% of those who do have a formal sales process report that it has a positive impact on sales performance.[1]

The first two numbers represent failure; however, the good news lies in the third number, which gives us a great clue as to how to solve the challenge.

Change the face of Sales and Marketing.

We can increase marketing and sales performance in several ways:

- Sales and marketing staffs should be in one department, and should work closely together on every step of the process, from understanding the customers to strategic marketing and sales planning and closing sales.

- Traditional sales compensation packages should reflect bottom lines and margins, and sales staff pay should be tied directly to the average margins achieved through their sales. Today, sales are usually judged on the basis of the revenues they bring in, which encourages discounting and lower margins.

- The first goal of sales representatives should be to provide solutions, rather than to sell a product or a service.

- Sales and marketing people should never promise anything that the business cannot deliver.

- Sales should be part of ongoing customer service and customer satisfaction. Working with the marketing staff, sales representatives should keep in touch with their customers.

When the First Impression
Is the Last Chance

In the chapter discussing Brands, we talked lots about the face of the brand, the impression that branding makes on people, and how that brand represents the perception people have of that face. When, where, and how your business touches people results in your brand perception or image.

Where does your business touch people more than in sales and marketing? Sales and marketing are about creating the first impression people have of your business. If it is a good impression, people might want a business relationship with you. On the other hand, if you create a bad impression, those same people might reject your products and services without ever learning more about them. Their first impression of the business will also be their last impression.

Instead of talking about bad impressions (which usually are caused by something we communicate verbally, pictorially, or physically), let's focus on what creates good impressions.

Your culture needs to be authentic; everything you do must be sincere. You must really care about people and their feelings. That is the essential ingredient for leading with the heart and for creating happiness. When you make people feel good about your company and about themselves, they want to work for you, they want to buy from you, and they want to spread the word about you.

They become your evangelizers. That is how you build Brand with a capital "B" and build relationships with people.

Feelings result in first impressions and perceptions. Your sales and marketing efforts should be directed at touching every one of these feelings: comfort, compassion, pride, sympathy, safety, curiosity, fascination, arousal, invigoration, passion, surprise, appreciation, encouragement, amusement, pleasure, satisfaction, relaxation, fulfillment, peace, tranquility, trust, serenity, rejuvenation, excitement, and happiness.

Sales people have direct contact with customers. They are in the best position to help customers make good decisions. If sales personnel do consulting well, they become trusted advisors. In this model, sales isn't about money. It is about service and building trusted relationships, with long-term value for the customer and increased marketing benefits for your business, your brand, and your bottom line.

Every person in the company represents the Brand, but sales people are the face of the Brand. So make sure each person represents the company's values and that everything they do is ethical.

Now, about those sales commissions: Instead of being rewarded for closing deals, your sales people should be rewarded for how many business relationships they build that are based on credibility, trust, honesty, values, ethics, and long-term value (sales) to the company. The bottom line will grow, and people at each end of the business relationship will sparkle with happiness.

Taking the Second Step

If sales and marketing personnel directly influence Brand image and all that that means, what is next? Assuming that you have followed the golden rule of building a successful culture and have the right people in the right role (including the head of marketing and a smart and savvy sales executive working hand-in-glove with him or her), they will be the first to lead the charge to find leads that breed sales.

In many organizations, sales and marketing staff act more like a bitter old married couple than a couple still enjoying their honeymoon. The marketing department is responsible for providing the sales department with leads. Sales people should be helping customers, not spending time looking for customers. If the leads they are getting are poor, the departments are not working together the way they should. That leads to a bad relationship between the two, and lower sales.

Marketing personnel must know their target audiences and frequently update the emotional and psychological characteristics that apply to that audience. If they work closely with sales personnel and ask the right questions, sales people will share what they know about their customers. The marketing department should then flesh out and refine its target lists to a manageable size for Sales by focusing only on the most valuable customers and clients.

When your customers are other businesses, marketers must identify the core decision makers within key target organizations: They need to know their names, what they read, what boards they sit on, their hobbies, and their sports interests. The more your marketing people learn about these key potential customers and clients, the better chance the Sales department has of building a sustainable and profitable relationship for both buyer and seller.

When the marketing staff has this kind of information, they can allocate their advertising and marketing outreach dollars wisely, because they know what that audience reads, what makes them tick, and how to touch their feelings as well as their intellect. They will be able to communicate in the buyer's language. This means advertising only in the publications their target audience reads, and only on the TV shows they watch. This means sending direct mail pieces (sales letters, brochures, postcards, and so on) only to those who are likely to pay attention and respond because the message resonates with their wants, needs, and desires.

No matter who your customers or clients are, marketing personnel need to understand the who and worry far less, if at all, about the what (products and services). The idea is to segment by buying habits and purchasing behaviors. Marketing ranks customers by their value, from 1 (extremely likely to buy and to buy often) to 5 (they wouldn't buy from us if we were the only game in town, or they buy products for rebates but return the product once the rebate check is cashed).

Here are some of the keys to a successful integrated sales and marketing campaign:

Sales and Marketing Tips

- Target your market based on key customers' behaviors, emotions, demographics, psychographics, and specific wants and needs.

- People choose products that work for them, resonate emotionally, and have personal meaning.

- The key to sales and marketing is to connect your products and services with what people want and need so that they tickle emotional and personal touch points.

- Know all about your customers and what will make them happy.

- What elicits the emotional, psychological, and intellectual responses that motivate people to buy from you and build a sustainable relationship with you?

- Identify what your individual customers' needs are, what their buying potential represents, and how they rank based on a scale that identifies their long-term value to you and your long-term value to them. Then segment them by buying habits and purchasing behaviors.

- Sales and marketing success is directly proportional to understanding customer needs, serving those needs, establishing relationships based on trust and credibility, and building, implementing, and managing happiness.

If you focus on the who instead of the what and develop an integrated campaign, your response rates will deliver return on your investment.

Maximizing Opportunities

Every business wants to conduct the most effective marketing campaign possible, but most businesses don't know enough about who buys and uses their products and services, what they use those products and services for, why they buy them in the first place, and, most important, why they buy them from any particular place.

What *usually* happens is that a company's marketing department creates attractive product packaging, but does not conduct research and customer satisfaction surveys. It collects names, but does not effectively build relationships with those customers. Most of the marketing pieces it sends out are ineffective, and the leads are weak.

Then the sales staff uses the same sales techniques for each customer, not taking into consideration that every person has unique purchasing characteristics. In this real-life scenario, the *who* is lost, and marketing and sales miss an opportunity to create a savvy plan that caters to the needs of individual customers and target groups.

To make sure the customers become and remain the top priority, discipline combined with proactive sales and marketing must drive marketing and sales.

Marketing to Deliver Results

CEOs and shareholders want more value for their money, and want it today. They are looking at marketing efforts critically. When the marketing department doesn't deliver results, it is viewed as not able to deliver value and seen as a wasted expense. But marketing should be the key to success. How does marketing deliver long-term results when short-term thinking is pushed down from the top?

There is no long-term business without long-term strategic thinking that produces short as well as long-term results. Marketing has to recognize this, accept it, and create strategies that deliver results today and tomorrow. Marketing efforts must be measurable, and they must build the business. We cannot expect business leaders to accept on faith that marketing is working. It must deliver real and measurable return on investment to the bottom line.

Like every other functional area of a business, analysis of marketing and sales expenditures has to be done first. Strategies that result in return on investment must be built into everything you do. Reduce your reliance on gut feelings, and invest in intelligence, research, analysis, and testing. Make sure all your goals are appropriate, realistic, and measurable, but do not abandon your commitment to people and their happiness.

In a meeting some years ago, I heard a CEO say, "We spend more money on IT than any other department, and I don't know what they do." Today, that same CEO would likely add marketing to the mix. Sharing colorful and complimentary brochures around the table and showing witty or humorous ads in the executive boardroom no longer cuts it. You had better be able to explain what your marketing spending achieves in real numbers. Your company's existence depends upon it.

A factor you need to consider when analyzing your return on investment is that you cannot measure short-term costs without measuring revenue over the lifetime of customers. There is lots of research to suggest that customer loyalty pays off big in the long-term, not only in sales to the loyal customer, but in sales to the customers who hear about the Brand from that loyal customer. The caveat here is that we need to be careful how we measure success. Focus long-term in everything you do, including cost analysis. We cannot measure expenditures without comparing the costs to the revenue. Return on investment is the correct measuring stick to use.

One of the secrets to positive growth is to stop patronizing people by producing products and services you *think* people want and then creating markets for them. Instead, go back to touching people by producing products and services that create experiences consumers want *and* need. Create a marketing culture that produces good competitive intelligence and excellent marketing research, and develop a relationship with your market.

Understanding Customers

Sales and marketing success is directly proportional to how well you understand customer needs, serve those needs, establish relationships based on trust and credibility, and build, implement, and increase happiness.

We must differentiate our customers and recognize that they are individuals who can be segmented into large audiences — but *only* if we understand what their needs are, what their buying potential represents, and how they rank based on a scale that identifies their long-term value to you and *your* long-term value to *them*.

You must meet your company's goals and your customers' needs. Both must show positive growth in order for your business to maximize its potential. It is not about what you think your customers need, and it is not about what you believe your company stands for. It comes down to what customers *think* they need and what they believe your company stands for. You must make positive customer connections, based on their emotional, psychological, and purchasing needs. You must understand each of those human traits as well as is possible to make those connections. Furthermore, you must be innovative and cost-effective. Then you will meet your company's goals and your customers' needs.

Allocate money to advertising, public relations, and direct marketing after first understanding who you are targeting; what those customers think and feel and need; what your value is to them; and what their value is to you. This requires analysis, intelligence, and research before you invest money in any aspect of marketing. Far too frequently, businesses think they need to advertise because everyone else does. And there are lots of advertising and marketing firms willing to spend a business's dollars. Before you spend money on any marketing effort, you must conduct a cost-benefit analysis first, and then allocate your dollars correctly.

Marketing can be expensive. Print and media advertising seldom produce a financial return equal to what is possible when money is invested in a carefully analyzed and constructed integrated marketing plan. But you won't know where to invest your money if you don't have a thorough understanding of the who, if you don't perform a deep analysis of your objectives, and if you don't run your numbers before committing to tactics.

What does a repeat customer look like?

You need to understand the difference between customer satisfaction and customer loyalty before you can create loyal customers.

Your goal should be to create great customer experiences, not customer satisfaction. Customers work hard to find companies that offer great experiences. Satisfaction seldom leads to customer loyalty, but great experiences do.

Measuring Customer Value

Marketing and sales costs tend to be higher when you are trying to expand your customer base. Returning and loyal customers do not cost as much to retain in terms of advertising. But in order to grow your business, you must constantly have new customers and retain them once you win them over.

Your measure of success is going to be how many new customers you win. You need to know how to measure new customer value. You must create new customer growth regularly, but you also must show a return on your investment.

Don Peppers and Martha Rogers explain that you need to gauge the return on the customer (ROC) to calculate the genuine cost and benefit of your acquisition program. "ROC is the metric you should use in order to choose which particular types of customers to try to acquire, given the expected acquisition cost and the immediate and future profit expected from them, because ROC measures the rate at which overall value is being created— considering both the current costs of your acquisition program and the changes in overall customer equity generated for your firm."

In other words, you need to understand the lifecycle value of new customers. Are they coming simply to take advantage of an offer, or do they offer long-term potential to your bottom line? By understanding their reasons for becoming first-time customers, you can evaluate your marketing and sales strategies to maximize your retention rates.

To gain a better understanding of their calculations, read Peppers and Rogers's 2005 article, "Customer Acquisition: How can executives measure new customer value?" published in *Return on Customer Monthly*. I'll leave the math to the experts and stay with the strategic and tactical importance of these ideas. Let me leave you with this thought from the article:

"You could easily think of a prospective customer as a customer with a great deal of growth potential. Your mission, as a business, is to realize some of that potential by changing the customer's otherwise expected future behavior."

Capturing Your Audience's Attention

One of a marketing department's most important jobs is cutting through all the noise of marketing and sales to grab your target audience's attention. Remember, just capturing their minds will not be enough to turn them into profitable and long-term customers. First buys are more emotional than intellectual, so you also must capture your audience's heart. Doing so requires vision, creativity, and innovation.

Toyota, for example, did not simply create a hybrid to combat escalating energy prices before energy costs began their ascent into the stratosphere in 2005. They built a cool car called the Prius that not only made good intellectual sense, but also appealed to emotion, resulting in purchase. Ford created a similar scenario and committed to building more hybrids.

But all is not automatically well when innovation and engineering combine to meet customers' needs. A Boston Consulting Group survey of 940 senior managers in 2005 found innovation was critical to financial success. However, more than 50 percent of those managers surveyed were not satisfied with their returns.

You must use market research to create better opportunities, innovate, and produce excellent returns on investment. All your functional areas must collaborate and align with your strategic plan. The marketing research must result in visionary thinking to create and deliver products and services that meet customers' needs in ways previously not done. Of course, if you do not have the right people in the right jobs working within the right culture, this won't happen.

Customer Service

I have talked about the impact that sales people have on Brand because they make the primary customer contacts. That also holds true for your Customer Call Center, whether it is you the sole proprietor, or you the executive who oversee a large corporation. Every consumer touch point affects the brand image.

When a customer calls your business, the person who answers the telephone must treat the customer as if he or she is your company's most important person at that moment. The caller must feel, upon hanging up, that you value his or her business and that you will do whatever it takes to make him or her happy. However, in many companies customer calls are all too often treated as unimportant. The customer who finds a way through a complicated, long, boring, and rude telephone maze often reaches a company rep who is difficult to communicate with and unable to solve the problem. That means more time on hold until another company rep comes on the line, asking the customer to go through the entire story again, before he or she can begin to address the issue, and maybe solve it.

Is this considerate customer service or relationship-building? Our reaction is usually "I'll never buy anything again from that business!"

This leaves a huge gap for some savvy businessperson to fill. To a great extent, this book is dedicated to filling that gap. If you can build a business based on values, leading with the heart, and happiness, you will take market share away from more-established and more-profitable businesses who don't really care for or respect the customer after the sale has been made. Not caring about the customer as much as the sale will eventually lead any business to shrinking margins and a disappearing bottom line.

Treat customers in ways that convince them that you appreciate and enjoy their business. You'll build a great Brand, increase sales and marketing opportunities, enhance customer trust and loyalty, and grow sales and margins.

Smart executives and entrepreneurs grab market share from businesses that outsource service overseas where language and cultures collide, use technology in place of human contact, and hire first-level service people who cannot solve a problem that is not written down in the service guide in front of them. More and more customers are seeking alternatives for their purchasing dollar.

Marketing departments are the key. They can conduct the research and gather intelligence to identify the gaps and fill those gaps. They can put the customer at the center of everything the business does. Marketing should be responsible for the strategy and the execution. The primary questions they must ask are:

1. What is the Brand image you want to build? How do you want customers to view your business?
2. How do you want that image communicated to customers?
3. How will that perception be reflected in every customer interaction with your company?

Forrester Research analyst Elana Anderson tells us that when a strong connection between marketing and the contact center does not exist, too much is left to chance. "When customers have a bad experience on the phone, that's a bad reflection on the brand."

Some experts and many businesses fail to recognize the need to align sales, marketing, and the call center. If you believe that customer touch points determine Brand image and you believe that those touch points are opportunities to build Brand and to make customers happy, loyal, and valuable to the bottom line, then you must build a business where sales, marketing, and the call center work closely together. That alignment and partnership will work best, I believe, if they work under the same roof with the same management so that changes in one functional area are also made in the others. And your Strategic Plan must reflect these changes.

To either make the change or to build your sales, marketing, and service areas in this manner to begin with, you must develop a Strategic Plan that recognizes the challenges.

Tips for Sales and Marketing Departments

- Marketing should consider goals as long-term challenges. Call centers need to see them as short-term.

- Marketing and Sales departments need to communicate daily with the call center (if not more frequently), especially regarding new offers or discounts.

- Lines of communication must be two-way, and always open.

- Strategies, goals, and metrics must be built after everyone's voice is heard.

- Everyone needs to buy into the key responsibility that the most-important goals are creating and building a profitable business based on values and happiness.

- Everyone must protect the Brand zealously. It must be a priority.

- Alignment must represent a true partnership of the functional areas.

- Rewards must be based on everyone's success, not on individual success. This might call for a new sales incentive package.

- Each functional area must be proactive and must avoid reactive behavior at every opportunity.

- Everyone must focus on people: employees and customers.

- Every functional area with solutions to customer problems must be rewarded for communicating those solutions to the marketing and sales departments and the call center.

- Integrate, integrate, and integrate!

- Align, align, and align!

- Never do anything to risk alienating an employee or a customer.

Customer Retention vs. Customer Acquisition

You've heard it before: To achieve success, you must focus on customer retention, as customer acquisition is far more costly and requires more time and work to turn new customers into repeat customers.

In his new book, *The Ultimate Questions: Driving Profits and True Growth,* customer loyalty expert Fred Reichheld believes that we must learn how to turn loyal customers into word-of-mouth. He cites Costco as a good example. This big-box store has grown to 45 million members, despite spending little on advertising and marketing. Reichheld sees quality customer service, which results in high-quality relationships, as the primary mover. He says most companies would focus on building excellent customer relations if it did not cost them anything. Not investing in customer relations saves money in the short term, he says, but those customers will spend far less with you in the future than a loyal customer will. Furthermore, short-term customers are "shopping the deal" and often are unwilling to pay for value, reducing your margins.

Loyal customers are more likely to respond positively to higher-priced products and to your marketing efforts, resulting in increased profits. They also cost your business less in the long run, as they are less likely to return products, more likely to pay for their purchases promptly, and show interest in the full range of your products and services. Again, the cost of retaining loyal customers is less than the cost of acquiring new ones.

In the long-term, loyal customers cost less to maintain and earn you higher profits. The data shows this time and time again.

Do your sales reps represent your brand?

I've spent lots of time discussing how to build the Brand from the inside out, and no one represents better the reasons for doing so than do your sales reps, as they are usually your first touch points with your customers and clients. Unfortunately, most companies fail the test.

Internal brand-building must be ongoing, and the messages you send must be clear, concise, and easy to remember. Your sales reps need to be thoroughly trained to communicate your messages clearly and concisely with one voice. Messages must be consistent across all marketing channels, internally and externally.

It is a good idea to conduct ongoing Brand training for all employees, but sales reps also should be tested regularly by their managers so you are sure that they understand the brand messages and are communicating them properly.

Furthermore, every employee, especially sales reps and the marketing staff, must thoroughly understand where the business is going, how it is going to get there, and what each person must do to support the process. Compensation should be based on the results they achieve in making the business's goals. Do not base compensation packages for sales reps on their individual sales revenues, which encourage and reward them for selling products and services at discounts, thus reducing your margins. Instead, base their goals on margins, and compensate them on how well they achieve their overall goals.

➲ Practical and Tactical Advice ⬳

The Marketing Plan

The marketing department's primary goal is to achieve a measurable level of sales, driven first and foremost by the annual Strategic Plan. When the marketing department creates an ongoing marketing plan in support of the business's Strategic Plan, it should be driven by measurable goals.

In my view, too many marketing plans use a shotgun approach, tossing money at every kind of tactic to see what works and what doesn't. Avoid that wasteful approach! Build your marketing plan on knowing the who. What does the audience look like? What do they think, feel, read, watch, and want?

Use strategies and tactics to reach each member of each target audience, and the marketing channels most likely to reach them. Then reach out to their needs using print, television, and radio advertising; direct marketing, e-mail marketing, online marketing, and telemarketing; cross-promotional strategic partnering; executive presentations; trade shows; newsletters, blogs, white papers, and published articles; design and packaging; and word-of-mouth marketing.

Once you understand how each target audience prefers to receive the information and what kinds of messages each will respond to, create marketing, public relations, and advertising communication specifically designed and written to appeal to their preferences. There is not one magical marketing strategy, just as one profile does not fit your entire audience.

Sample Plan

According to the Direct Marketing Association's 2006 Response Rate Trends Report, telephone and e-mail produce the highest response rates (2.60% and 2.45%, respectively, in 2006) among direct marketing media channels for generating leads (direct mail pulled 1.27%).

If you think a direct mail campaign is simply sending out a postcard or a sales letter and then waiting for the telephone to ring, your efforts will fail. Like all marketing tools, direct marketing is most successful when used in an integrated campaign that is narrowly focused.

Here is an actual direct marketing plan for a high-tech business that wanted to co-market with a manufacturer and supplier of tablet PCs. The plan is simple in its concept, yet it contains the elements necessary to provide a suitable example. It supports and is aligned with the company's Strategic Plan.

Strategic Plan

Goals: What success will look like in units sold.

1. 20 docking stations
   (assuming a 40 percent sales on 50 telemarketing leads)
2. 100 Tablets
   (assuming 40 percent sales on 50 telemarketing leads)

Target Market: Healthcare organizations adopting and/or launching Electronic Medical Records (EMR); Hospitals (Chief Medical Officers, Chief Nursing Officers and CIOs); Ambulatory Care and Clinics

Unique Value Proposition: XYZ companies have worked together to develop and offer the only tablet solution that creates a system for secure storage and charging of your tablet PCs. No other tablet features this solution.

Strategies and Tactics:

- *Configure pricing* (manager names)
- *Develop reseller list and strategy* (manager names)
- *Marketing tactics:*
  - Develop e-mail copy, sales letter copy, postcard copy, and one four-color collateral piece. Target date and responsibility: early to mid-September (manager names)
  - Purchase distribution list for direct mail to target market, if unable to use ABC's list for e-mail campaign. Target date and responsibility: mid-September (manager names)
  - E-mail campaign using XYZ's distribution list. Target date and responsibility: mid-to late September (manager names)
  - Print and mail sales letter and collateral piece. Target date and responsibility: early October (manager names)
  - Update Web site content. Target date and responsibility: early October (manager names)

(continued)

Strategic Plan *(concluded)*

Strategies and Tactics (continued)

- Print and mail postcard. Target date and responsibility: late October (manager names)
- Follow-up telephone calls. Target date and responsibility: November and December (hire a telemarketing company, calling to be managed by manager names)
- Follow-up sales calls on leads. Target date and responsibility: November, December, and continuing, if necessary, to follow up on leads generated by telemarketing (manager names)

Budget:

• Marketing consultant	$2,500.00
• Distribution list for three-time use	2,803.14
• Collateral design: Sales letter, collateral piece, postcard	1,250.00
• Direct Mail services include postage, stuffing, and mailing; Printing includes envelopes, sales letter, collateral piece, postcard (two mailings, 2,000 each)	2,911.00
• Telemarketing – 2,000 calls	6,200.00
Total Budget	$15,664.14

Marketing Communications

The only secret handshake you need know is that marketing is all about communication. You speak and your audience listens, but they will only listen if you speak to them about things they care about in ways that resonate with them, and through tools that they are likely to respond to.

Therefore, marketing communications should:

- Represent the Brand in the ways you want your customers and clients to perceive it.

- Be 100 percent accurate and clear.

- Tap into the emotions and the intellect of potential customers and clients.

- Clearly and concisely state and show the benefits and values of the products and services you deliver.

- Tell and show the audience why they should purchase from you. What separates your business from all the others offering the same products and services?

- Tell and show customers and clients what to do next (i.e., call an 800 number, send in the attached coupon, etc.).

Word-of-Mouth Marketing

Give customers, clients, consultants, and business writers reasons to talk about your business and your products and services! You need to create buzz and word-of-mouth marketing (which may be the best marketing and sales tool available). When others spread the word about your business, it helps you achieve the goals and objectives stated within your business, marketing, and sales plans.

In the past, marketers assumed that when people were happy with your business, they would spread the word. They did not fully understand how they could encourage and manage word-of-mouth marketing.

Today, many businesses work hard to make people happy. They listen to people, respond to their needs, wants, and desires, and communicate in the right way at the right time. Word-of-mouth marketing recognizes that positive buzz builds a business and negative buzz hurts it. When you use word-of-mouth marketing, you . . .

* Educate people about the value of your products and services.

* Educate and inform them about the values inherent within your Brand.

* Identify and communicate with people who are most likely to talk about your business.

* Provide the tools necessary to make it easy for people to share your information (e.g., an e-mail that can be easily forwarded, informational reports that can be shared).

* Take advantage of what you have learned about how and when people share information about your business.

* Listen and respond to what people are saying, whether it is positive or negative. You give them a free voice.

You can and should influence and encourage word-of-mouth marketing.

Referrals and Leads

Word-of-mouth marketing represents a good way to get referrals and leads. For the purposes of this discussion, a referral happens when someone gives you the contact information of an individual or business they think is interested in your products or services or connects you with someone who can help your business grow in other ways. A lead refers to the contact information of someone who is very likely interested in your products or services.

Sales depend on referrals and leads. Nourish a system to deliver the referrals and leads: word-of-mouth marketing, networking, direct marketing that requests referrals and leads from people familiar with your business, event marketing, and so on. Reward those customers and clients who pass along referrals and leads that result in business growth.

Advertising and what it means to you.

When a business wants to get the word out about their company or a new offer, it usually turns to advertising first. Never spend money on any form of marketing, including advertising, until you have done your home-work! At the very least, you must know the answers to these questions before you purchase any advertising:

- What is the purpose of the advertising? Is it Brand building? An offer for a discounted product or service? To announce a new product? Or is it something else?

- What is your budget, and what will that budget buy?

- What will be your return on investment, and how will you measure it?

- What media will keep you within budget and produce your minimum return on investment? And what are your risks of failure and your chances of success?

It also is a good idea to know and to understand what other businesses are doing. Where are they spending their advertising dollars?

In January of 2006, information industry research firm Outsell Inc. reported on a survey it conducted of 625 U.S. advertisers, that found that online ad budgets made up 18 percent of respondents' total advertising budgets, compared with 16 percent of their budgets in 2005. Results can be tracked easily, and advertisers want results—they don't really care where their dollars are spent, as long as they return results. This is why online advertising continues to grow.

Researching data about advertising expenditures is not a difficult task. Much of the research can be accomplished quickly online, so if you cannot afford sophisticated research done by experts, make sure you at least do some research on your own before you spend even a dime on a marketing tool.

Direct Mail That Works

Like any marketing tool, direct mail succeeds only when it is people-centered, focused, and carefully planned, and it uses best practices and innovation. Remember, a direct-mail campaign is not simply mailing a postcard: It is a well-planned strategy that is phased in over several months. It usually includes an initial mailing of a sales letter and the offer, followed up by one or two additional mailings of information that your readers care about and that help them understand why they should care about the offer; perhaps an e-mail to an opt-in list; and a post-card reminder.

According to a report from the Direct Marketing Association, direct marketing sales are expected to grow by 6.4 percent annually through 2009, compared with overall U.S. sales growth estimates of 4.8 percent.

The association also reported that, direct marketing ad expenditures account for 47.9 percent of total advertising spending. According to its report, direct mail ($49.8 billion) and telephone marketing ($47 billion) currently represent the most popular direct marketing channels.

What are your expectations from direct mail? According to the association, direct mail response rates range from 0.03 percent to 15 percent. You should try to get a response rate closer to 15 percent than 0.03 percent. So how do you do that?

Tips on Using Direct Mail

Before you use direct-mail marketing, here are a few tips to help you get good results:

1. Begin by identifying your purpose. Are you brand-building, selling, announcing, or presenting an offer customers can't refuse?

2. Develop a measurable goal and metrics to track your level of success.

3. Then identify the audience most likely to respond to your direct-mail piece. Create your "leads" distribution list by purchasing a list or by developing one in-house.

4. Qualify your leads by understanding your audience, down to the smallest detail possible. At the very least, make sure the names and addresses on your list are as accurate as possible.

5. Determine the formats most likely to appeal to your list (e.g., e-mail, postcard, sales letter, packaging, and so on). All formats average about the same response rate, when the appropriate format is chosen. The wrong format drives the response rate downward.

Here are my thoughts about each medium and how you might use it:

1. Postcards are most successful when you want to make an initial contact with a potential client. Your best chance for good return is when the offer includes something tangible.

(continued)

Tips on Using Direct Mail *(concluded)*

2. Letters are best used with potential customers and clients who have shown some interest in your business, perhaps by downloading a report or asking for more information from you.

3. Two-dimensional and three-dimensional packages that are colorful and that use unusual shapes generate the most interest, but they can cost 300−400% more than letters and postcards. They must be used carefully and with fully qualified lists.

4. E-mail is the least expensive medium, but has the most downsides. To stay within the law, your list must be opt-in: every name on the list must have already agreed to receive e-mailings from you. But even then, SPAM and Phishing filters will catch many of your e-mails before they reach their destination.

At the end of the day, your most important direct-mail message is the offer. It can be a discounted product or service, a free demonstration or consultation, a free article that can be downloaded from your Web site, a free gift, and so on.

To achieve the highest response rate, you must create a minimum of three impressions in the recipients' minds, and you must follow up with each recipient after those three impressions are made. That is why a combination of the tools, used in separate mailings, work best.

Sales: How to Avoid Discounting

Good and great companies don't sell price—they sell value. Still, too many businesses approach a sale as if it is combat between the seller and the buyer, with the seller having to win at all costs. This attitude frequently ends up with the seller offering a discount if the individual agrees to purchase the product or service. This results in two things: deep discounts to close the deal, and razor-thin margins that can ultimately mean the death of your business.

When I hear sales people say "In this industry, people buy price," I want to scream at them "They buy price because you *sell* price!" If you learn only one thing from this book, it should be that everything a business does—especially sales—is about people, and few people buy only price. Instead, they buy benefits, resources, service, timing, status, relationships, trust, credibility, happiness, value, and solutions.

Obviously, if they can get those things *and* a good price, they will. However, what sales should do instead is approach every customer and client as a consultant whose job is to solve problems and ease people's stress by providing tools and services that address their customers' and clients' needs. The "combat" attitude often built into sales isn't always the sales person's fault. In fact, usually it is management's problem, because management created a compensation package that rewards revenues instead of profits. Until that changes, sales people will continue to offer discounts.

Quick Tips to Increase Sales

- Understand your customer's business, needs, and wants before your first meeting.

- Know as much as possible about the person you plan to meet with, so you can begin building a relationship with him or her.

- Approach the sales meeting as if you are a consultant whose job it is to help people solve problems: Your ultimate goal is to become a trusted advisor. Your job is not to make money; it is to help people solve problems.

- Show up fully prepared for your meetings with potential customers and clients. Know their business as well as you know your own. Check out their Web site and their annual report, and talk to people who know something about the company.

- Always promise less than you think you can offer. If you meet expectations, you provide good customer service. If you exceed expectations, you and your company are heroes.

- Listen more than you talk.

- Be 100 percent honest, 100 percent of the time. Always sell solutions, not tools. And always sell value, not price.

- Recognize that you may not have a product or service that will solve the problem, even though you think you do when you set up the meeting. Be aware that buyers already have spent lots of time trying to solve the problem in-house. Learn what has already been done before you offer a solution.

- Listen, listen, and listen! Ask the right questions. Gain an understanding of your customer's specific needs. Understand the systems in place that likely will affect the performance of your product or service. (Your product or service might not be compatible with the in-house systems, causing more problems and financial stress than originally existed.)

(continued)

Quick Tips to Increase Sales *(concluded)*

- Always be aware that you are the face of your company's Brand. Treat this responsibility with the respect and dignity it deserves. You are the "brand ambassador," first and foremost.

- Offer the right solution at the right time, and never sell anything that won't solve the customer's problem. That's right—sometimes you will need to tell the potential buyer that you can't help them, and you will have to recommend someone else who can. (By doing so, you have gained the respect of that buyer for life, and you will reap the rewards of that in future sales, to that buyer and to all those to whom he tells the story about the sales person who walked away.)

- Undersell and over-deliver.

- Focus on the results of the interaction from the buyer's point of view. Follow up to see how the buyer is doing and how your product or service is performing.

- Most important: You must care deeply about your Brand, the values it represents, all the people (customers or not), and happiness.

Sample Sales Letter

People often ask me how a sales letter should be written. I think there are several good ways to create a sales letter. Here is an example.

Great Headline
Great Sub Head

Dear so and so:

Do you want to grow your business? **Here's how we will meet your needs:**

- You talk, we listen, and then we return with strategies that meet your wants and needs.
- You grow your business with marketing, advertising, public relations, employee communication, and graphic design services customized just for you.
- You get noticed.
- You get customers.

To get an edge and focus on what works, call 555-555-555.

From zero net revenues to profitable in four months!

In the fall of 2006, a start-up asked us to submit a proposal to help launch their business. After interviewing more than a few marketing firms, they hired [your company name]. We started by asking lots of questions: But the most important was "What do you want your business to look like in six months, a year, and five years?" With the answers to those questions, we built a marketing plan that could be executed in five months, from idea to end of launch. At the end of the fourth month, the client brought in enough business to cover its marketing costs and make a profit.

[Your company name] grows your business. And you are treated as if you are our only client. **Call l 555-555-555.**

[Include a few third-party testimonials here.]

Sincerely yours,

Name and title

The takeaways are that it is short, it begins with a headline created to grab the reader's interest, it has the reader's name, it talks about what the customer will get, it provides evidence that you have experience getting what the customer wants, it includes the action item (the telephone number to call), and it ends with several third-party testimonials, testifying to your company's good work.

This is one example of a sales letter that works. Take time to personalize your letter, communicate what you offer, and make it as perfect as you can before you send it to anyone.

Points to Ponder

- Sales and marketing departments must care about people and their needs and share the information people will need to make good choices about products and services. This is what we define as leading with the heart and creating happiness.

- Sales and marketing are the two most important functions within a business.

- The face of sales and marketing changes when people come first.

- Sales and Marketing usually create the first impression people have of a business. If it is a good impression, people are likely to want a business relationship with you, assuming you offer what they need.

(continued)

Points to Ponder *(continued)*

- We all react to other people and their products and services with our emotions. Research shows that people choose products that work for them: products that resonate emotionally and that have personal meaning.

- You must really care about people and their feelings. When you make people feel good, they will want to work for you, buy from you, and spread the word about you. That is how you build Brand with a capital "B": by building relationships one at a time.

- Sales people touch customers directly, which puts them in the best position to help clients make good decisions. If they do this well, your sales personnel will become trusted advisors. In this model, a sale isn't about money; it is about service.

- Businesses don't know enough about the people who buy their products and services and what they use those products and services for. They also don't know why they buy them in the first place, and most important, why they buy them from any particular place. You need to find these things out!

- Marketing and sales are about communicating the right message, the right way, to the right customer.

(continued)

Points to Ponder *(continued)*

- Do your marketing and sales homework before you spend any money in these areas, rather than make decisions with your gut.

- Strategies that result in return on investment must be built into everything you do. Invest in intelligence, research, analysis, and testing, and make sure all goals are appropriate, realistic, and measurable.

- Stay focused on people and on the long term.

- It is not about what you think your customers need. It is about *what they think they need*. It is not about what you believe your Brand stands for. It is about *what customers believe* your Brand stands for.

- Marketing and selling to new customers generally costs more than marketing and selling to returning and loyal customers.

- Although you must create new customer growth regularly, doing so must show a return on your investment, both in the short and the long term.

- One of the marketing department's most important jobs is cutting through all the noise to grab your target audience's attention. Just capturing their minds will not be enough to turn them into profitable and long-term customers.

- First buys are more emotional than intellectual.

(continued)

Points to Ponder *(concluded)*

- Capture your audience's heart. This will require vision, creativity, and innovation.

- If you believe that customer touch points determine Brand image and that your primary responsibility is to build the Brand and to make customers happy, loyal, and valuable to the bottom line, then you must build a business where sales, marketing, and the call center work closely together to help make those things happen

Chapter Nine
Doing the Right Thing

Employees, customers, and communities that care little whether or not your business survives and prospers threaten its existence. When you lead with the heart, execute strategies with passion, and build happiness, you achieve engagement: People will start to care about your business, and will want you to do well.

When people don't care one way or the other, you'll experience losses in productivity, little customer loyalty, shrinking market share, and difficulty attracting quality employees and valuable customers. Business models that are driven by greed and executives who either don't know how or don't want to change create this kind of apathy. According to a recent Gallup poll, 55 percent of employees are doing the bare minimum required of their jobs, and 19 percent are actively working to sabotage your business. That leaves just 26 percent of employees who care.

Attitudes are deeply imbedded within organizational cultures, so the challenges are greater for well-established businesses that want to become more people-centered than for newer businesses built from the inside out.

The good news for those suffering from this form of myopia (in which vision begins and ends at the cash register) is that leading with the heart can change even the worst of cultures and help engage employees and customers so that they care about your success.

The new vision I write about here is a vision conceived and practiced by individuals who can see a great future for their company. If the vision is nurtured with passion, it has a solid chance of success.

From Passion to a Solid Foundation

When the business is in its infancy, the proud parents who understand the essentials of success raise their prodigy on these fundamental principles:

1. Make values and goals the backbone of your business.

2. Innovate and encourage your people to express their ideas, opinions, and perspectives, and reward them when their thoughts benefit your business.

3. Make respect, dignity, trust, and credibility part of everything your business says and does.

4. Promote an environment where people can question authority. You will be pleasantly surprised by the results.

5. Spread the passion among your employees by regularly demonstrating and communicating this passion. Let them know they are the most important part of your business — not revenues, not products, not services, but *people.*

Companies that put people first and are passionate about leading with the heart and giving employees opportunities to share in the decision making tell their people that *they* are the reason for their company's success, and they mean it.

Let's spend some time now discussing how you spread that passion the right way, beyond the business itself.

Spreading Passion beyond the Corporate Hallways

Jim Collins backs up his business advice with extensive research from the real world, and melds this with common sense. He writes about the importance of passion and what he calls the "hedgehog concept," which is illustrated by intersecting circles containing these three concepts: what you are deeply passionate about; what you can be best at in the world; and what drives your economic engine.

Collins says you need all three concepts to move a company from good to great. The point I like the best is that passion alone won't result in a prosperous and growing business. You might make lots of money doing what you are doing, but if you don't have the potential to be the best in the world, your company cannot move beyond successful to great. Going from good to great is about maximizing your potential and always working to become great.

As most great leaders come to understand, you cannot create or motivate passion. You either have it for what you do and what you create, or you don't. Successful business leaders and entrepreneurs hire the right people for the right job—that is, people who carry the passion gene. During the interview process, the people who seem to possess a zest for life and passion for their work stand out as individuals who will be passionate about their work and passionate about their company. When a company lives its principles in everything they do and say, most of its employees will be passionate about the company.

Collins puts it this way: "The good-to-great companies did not say, 'Okay, folks, let's get passionate about what we do.' Sensibly, they went the other way entirely: We should only do those things that we can get passionate about."

Leadership Does Matter

Superstar CEOs don't seem to make much of a difference in a company's performance, but leadership matters. I once heard leaders described as "people who leave their footprints in their areas of passion." Those footprints are large and impressive, and they are made by people we want to be around and follow. Such leaders are never satisfied. They are charismatic. They care about people, and their businesses are nearly always in pursuit of excellence. True leaders are in a constant state of reinvention. They embrace change. They understand that passion must be nourished and innovation must be encouraged. They surround themselves with smart people, and they reward excellence at every level. They are leaders and managers, and they know when to do both—they lead people and manage processes.

Great leaders are passionate, visionary, creative, self-disciplined, organized, fair, open-minded, smart, social, moral, ethical, and honest. Real leaders maintain a healthy tension between logic and passion, and they are terrific communicators. Most important, they recognize their strengths and weaknesses, and they work within their area of passion.

It's all about the team.

Great leaders hire great people who share many of the same qualities that make the CEO a person to respect and follow. And those people are also passionate about what they do and hire great people who possess at least some of those qualities. Together, they form the team that drives success and works diligently toward greatness.

Through complete and frequent communication, members of the team always know where the team is going, how they will measure goals so they know where they are on the journey, and how to recognize success. Each member of the team brings their passion to bear on what they do best. Because of the culture they work in, they know they can take calculated risks and be innovative without fear of being reprimanded or fired. They also know that they can use their skills and strengths to implement best practices, without fear of not fitting in with the creative side of the team.

A great team melds individual competencies, skills, strengths, and passion to achieve success. Each member has his or her own sense of business logic, and applies it within their area of expertise. Members communicate well, and are not fearful of either success or failure. The team expects to be rewarded based on its contributions to the business goals. Like the business, each individual and each team works toward long-term goals, but understands and appreciates the need for lots of short-term achievements. Within each team, leaders stand out and are looked to for their leadership.

The team and the culture work because leaders don't over-manage. The employees are free to do what they do best within a business culture that encourages it. Such an environment brings out the best in people, resulting in many successes, a few failures, and a business driven toward greatness.

This kind of passion and the culture that it produces reaches far beyond the hallways of corporate headquarters. It extends to each store, each distribution center, each plant, and each warehouse to replicate itself over and over again.

Employees, consumers, and the community all benefit from this passion for employee and customer experiences that create happiness, and passion for products and services that work for people and that exceed their expectations.

➲ Practical and Tactical Advice ᗡ

Values sprinkled with passion make a difference.
Despite the headlines being made by some unethical characters, anyone who studies the business world will see that higher standards for performance, morals, and ethics are being applied to financial decisions. Some of this is due to regulations such as Sarbanes Oxley, but much of it exists because companies are beginning to see

Practical and Tactical Advice *(continued)*

themselves as an important part of their communities and of the U.S. As these companies begin to make decisions by putting people first and foremost, they see the positive effects that this has on their business and their community. They then begin to act differently and more responsibly.

Business ethics based on our core values are about much more than simply making amends for our sins. They are about striving for excellence, building trust and credibility with all stakeholders (including non-shareholders), building authentic and pleasurable people experiences, and they are about increased profits.

Striving to do the right thing and always working toward excellence inevitably leads to increased market share and sales.

Wrongdoing destroys health, wealth, and the world. Doing the right thing enhances health, wealth, and the world.

Ethics-based businesses built on values and passion head off trouble, reduce monies spent fixing those troubles, and inspire employees and consumers to want to associate with them. They contribute positively to the environment, treat people well, and are honest and fair in their communication, financial affairs and pricing, and treatment of all people.

The public expects businesses to be held to a higher standard than at any previous time in history. Corporate wrongdoing ultimately ends up as public information, and the public wants to see the wrongdoers punished for their deeds. It is imperative, from a practical point of view, and as business owners that you always act with integrity and require everyone we employ to do so as well.

Of course, if you subscribe to the principles of leading with your heart and what I sometimes call the "happiness quotient," your organization will not need to worry about wrongdoing, because you will have prepared it for excellence by laying a foundation of values and concern for and about people. Your business will automatically do the right thing, and it will succeed.

Here is some good news: More and more business leaders in the U.S. and in other countries are trying to develop companies with high ethical standards, companies that are built on business models that look very much like the one I am writing about. They seek excellence in everything and every group of people they serve: investors, customers, employees, and the public.

What does doing the right thing look like?

In August of 2001, Baxter International's chairman and CEO Harry M. Jansen Kraemer, Jr. received disturbing news: Several dialysis patients in Spain had died. Baxter International, a medical equipment and supplies manufacturer, had made one of the filters for the dialysis machine those patients were using.

The company worked with an independent testing company to test the filters, and found nothing wrong. Unfortunately, shortly thereafter, several more dialysis patients died while being treated in Croatia. Baxter International re-tested the equipment and discovered that the testing procedure being used was flawed. Fluid used in the dialysis process that was made by another company turned to gas in the bloodstream, which in some circumstances can cause pulmonary embolisms.

Some might think those findings relieved Baxter International of primary responsibility for the death of those patients. Not Kraemer. Instead, he recommended that the board of directors reduce his 2001 bonus by 40 percent and the bonuses of other executives by 20 percent because he believed that ultimately they are responsible for results. Furthermore, Baxter International issued a public apology, shut down the plants that made the products in question, and settled with the harmed families.

That is what doing the right thing looks like.

Fewer than 10 percent of executives interviewed in a 2006 study by Boston College's Center for Corporate Citizenship believe that their greatest duty is only to create wealth for investors. The rest believe that businesses must be concerned about protecting the environment and supporting the needs of their employees. CEOs from companies as diverse as GE, IBM, Raytheon, Ernst & Young, Nestle, Apache Oil, and Timberland talked in their interviews about how they manage their companies and respond to the growing number of societal issues and vocal stakeholders.

Doing good reaps great rewards.

The reward for good work is that people will thank you for doing the right thing. As I've maintained throughout this book, those who work only for profit may survive and even experience some success, but they will never maximize the potential of the human energy within their company or the human capital outside their company — people who might purchase their products and services or invest in their stock — if profit is all they care about.

Employees do their best and are most innovative and productive when treated with respect, dignity, and honesty. Customers spend more on your products and services when your good works exceed their expectations and create happy experiences. And all shareholders invest more with you when you are honest with them. If you energize and engage your employees, excite and impress your customers, give back to your community, and are always honest with all your stakeholders, you will sleep better at night, feel better about yourself, attract great people to your side, and increase your business's profits the right way, while maximizing the potential of your business.

All this is backed up by research, but most of it just makes sense. Who doesn't want to be associated with good things? People who care more about money than good things are a risk inside any business culture because of what they might do to co-workers or to your business to get that money. My conclusions, and I hope yours, are to do the right thing and reap the rewards of doing so.

Points to Ponder

The fundamentals of any business are values, goals, innovation, respect, dignity, trust, credibility, openness, and passion.

- Make values and goals the backbone of your business.
- Innovate by encouraging people to express their ideas, opinions, and perspectives. Reward them when their thoughts benefit your business.
- Build respect, dignity, trust, and credibility into everything your business says and does.
- Promote an environment where people can question authority: you will be pleasantly surprised by the results.
- Spread passion throughout your workforce by letting people know all the time that they are the most important part of your business—not revenues, not products, not services, but people.
- Great leaders are passionate, visionary, creative, self-disciplined, organized, fair, open-minded, smart, social, moral, ethical, and honest.
- Great leaders hire great people who share many of the same qualities that make the CEO a person to respect and follow.
- Teams must make the most of individual competencies, skills, strengths, and passion. Each member should have his or her own sense of business logic and apply it to their own area of expertise. Individuals must communicate well as a team, and not be fearful of success or failure.

Chapter Ten
Making a Difference

Defining Corporate Social Responsibility

Business for Social Responsibility was founded in 1992 to help all companies achieve success in ways that demonstrate respect for values, ethics, people, communities, and the environment.[1] In fact, this is how the organization defines corporate social responsibility. This definition fits well within the philosophy underpinning the focus of this book: to lead with your heart and to create happiness.

What's in it for the bottom line?

Presidents, CEOs, and CFOs have a responsibility to their boards and to shareholders to deliver profits. When businesses are people-focused rather than profit-focused, they will not only be able to fulfill their fiduciary responsibility to grow profits and their businesses, but their financial performance will actually be better than those businesses whose focus is primarily on profits.

Here are *Business Ethics Magazine*'s ten Best Corporate Citizens for 2007:

1. Green Mountain Coffee Roasters
2. Advanced Micro Devices
3. NIKE
4. Motorola
5. Intel Corp.
6. International Business Machines (IBM)
7. Agilent Technologies
8. Timberland
9. Starbucks
10. General Mills

Some of the other high-profile companies in the Top 100 are Dell, Cisco Systems, Johnson & Johnson, Kimberley-Clark, The Gap, Google, Southwest Airlines, and UPS.

Improving Financial Performance

Business and investment professionals have long debated whether or not there is a real connection between socially responsible business practices and positive financial performance. An increasing number of studies have been conducted to examine this link. Cone Corporate Citizenship Study for 2004 research, conducted over an especially long period of time (ten years) revealed that 80% of Americans trust companies that work for good causes, a 21% increase since 1997.[2]

"Our report is the nation's longest study of American attitudes toward corporate support of social issues," says Carol Cone, CEO of Cone, a Boston-based strategic marketing firm. "This study, in a series of research spanning over a decade, shows that in today's climate, more than ever before, companies must get involved with social issues in order to protect and enhance their reputations."

On the flip side, the research found that Americans generally react negatively to companies that behave illegally or unethically. Those surveyed said they would likely respond in a variety of ways:

- 90% would consider switching to another company's products or services.
- 81% would speak out against that company among family and friends.
- 80% would consider selling their investments in the company's stock.
- 80% would refuse to invest in that company.
- 75% would refuse to work at that company.
- 73% would boycott that company's products or services.
- 67% would be less loyal if employed by such a company.

Some companies aggressively communicate their efforts toward corporate citizenship. Others are reluctant, considering this boastful. But 86% of the individuals surveyed want companies to talk about their efforts.

"These facts, side-by-side, are a mandate," says Cone. "For senior executives, they are a mandate for action on social issues. For marketing executives, they are a license to communicate the company's commitment and efforts."

When communicating the good they do, business needs to understand which sources of information are the most credible, Cone's research indicates that the most-believed sources are family and friends (59%), government agencies (38%), news organizations (37%), the Internet (31%), religious organizations (29%), charities (26%), and the company itself (23%).

Business leaders need to understand what customers are thinking if they are to meet their wants and needs. Cone's research showed what Americans most value:

- Quality of products and services (98%)
- Fair-priced products and services (97%)
- Employee benefits (93%)
- Laws and regulations (93%)
- Human rights and manufacturing (93%)
- Support of a social issue (80%)

In short, Americans don't just want businesses to communicate about their good works; they want businesses to walk the talk. This is particularly true about young Americans who are significantly more likely to consider a company's citizenship practices when making purchasing, employment, and investment decisions.

"Today's young adults have learned to become savvy consumers, and have recognized the importance of a company standing for something that they believe in," says Cone. "Our research shows that cause-related activities will influence not only their buying habits, but also gain their loyalty and trust. Aligning with a cause is a significant strategy for companies to attract consumers and a future workforce at an early age and gain a long-term, sustainable competitive advantage."

The CEO of salesforce.com had this to say at the 2007 annual meeting of the Committee to Encourage Corporate Philanthropy:

"Employee empowerment is critical. Companies that rally employees around programs that make a difference in the world are going to secure more loyalty and value from them. Our employees know that this is a priority from the top and we lead by example," said Marc Benioff.

Reducing Operating Cost

Some corporate social responsibility initiatives can reduce operating costs dramatically. Many recycling programs cut waste-disposal costs and generate income by selling recycled materials. In the human resources arena, flexible scheduling and other work-life programs that result in reduced absenteeism and increased retention of employees often save companies money through increased productivity and reduction of hiring and training costs.

A 2007 report by global management consulting firm A.T. Kearney, of a study it conducted with the Institute for Supply Management (ISM), stated that almost 60% of North American companies have a sustainability strategy, and about 36% have a formal sustainability strategy for the supply management organization.[3]

Some of the companies reported that they are already beginning to see the financial benefits of sustainability, such as increased customer demand for sustainable products, improved employee morale, greater brand strength, and enhanced marketing opportunities for environmentally friendly products.

"Supply management organizations should not only focus on being compliant with new green standards. They can also pro-actively engage the supply base to drive sustainability-related innovations that can lead to pricing premiums and access to new markets," explained Daniel Mahler, A.T. Kearney vice president and leader of the Sustainability Study.

Enhancing Brand Image and Reputation

Customers often are drawn to brands and companies with a track record of social responsibility A company considered socially responsible has an enhanced reputation with the public, as well as an enhanced reputation within the business community. This increases its ability to attract capital and trading partners.

A 2001 corporate responsibility study showed that 61% of people surveyed who own stock said they had bought or sold shares on the basis of a company's social performance.

Another Cone Survey, this one conducted in March of 2007, reports that 32% of Americans who responded are more interested in the environment than they were a year ago. Most important, 93% believe companies have a responsibility to help preserve the environment.[4]

The study also revealed that 47% of respondents report that they have purchased environmentally friendly products, 21% have donated to an environmental organization, and 18% have advocated for environmental issues. In their own lives, 93% are conserving energy, 89% are recycling, 86% are conserving water, and 70% are telling family and friends about environmental issues.

With this information in hand, businesses better understand how to meet the wants, needs, and desires of their customers, while doing good works.

Increasing Sales and Customer Loyalty

A number of studies, including those I have already mentioned, suggest that there is a large and growing market for the products and services of companies perceived to be socially responsible. While businesses must first satisfy such key buying criteria as price, quality, availability, safety, and convenience, studies also show a growing desire to buy (or not buy) because of other values-based criteria, such as "sweatshop-free" and "child-labor-free" clothing, lower environmental impact, and absence of genetically-modified materials or ingredients.

"Americans clearly have a heightened environmental consciousness, and their expectations now touch on a range of business practices," explains Mike Lawrence, executive vice president of Corporate Responsibility at Cone. "Companies need to have a credible environmental strategy that reaches across their operations if they expect to secure consumer trust and loyalty."

Referring again to the 2007 Cone Consumer Environmental Survey, 91% of those in the study said that they have a more positive image of a company when it is environmentally responsible, and 85% said that they would consider switching to another company's products or services because of a company's negative corporate responsibility practices.

The environmentally-friendly products Americans in the survey say they buy are:

> - Products with recycled content (62%).
>
> - Cleaning supplies (48%).
>
> - Organic or other third-party certified foods/beverages (24%).
>
> - Energy-efficient cars (13%).
>
> - Green apparel (10%)
>
> 56% say that they are making energy-efficient home improvements.

Many Americans say they are willing to pay more for environmentally-friendly products because they will be saving money in the long-term, the products are readily and conveniently available, and they want to improve the health and welfare of future generations.

Going back to earlier but relevant research, a 2001 Hill & Knowlton/Harris Interactive poll reported that 79% of Americans surveyed take corporate citizenship into account when deciding whether or not to buy a particular company's product, and 36% said that they consider corporate citizenship an important factor when making purchasing decisions.

Increasing Productivity and Quality

Corporate efforts to improve working conditions, lessen environmental impacts, and increase employee involvement in decision making often lead to increased productivity and reduced error rate. For example, companies that improve working conditions and labor practices among their suppliers often experience a decrease in merchandise that is defective or that can't be sold.

"Connecting People to What Matters" from Deloitte Research reports that connecting your employees to people, purpose, and resources might improve an organization's productivity, innovation, and growth.[5]

"Our corporate culture is based on trust between employees, customers, and the company," said Jeff Chambers, vice president of Human Resources for the airline SAS. "We care about employees' personal and professional growth, which inspires them to do great work. Employees who solve our clients' biggest problems yield happy, committed customers. It isn't altruism. It's good business."

Although the report talks about how technology can be both a distraction and an asset, it is easy to see that human connections are important. What better way to connect your employees than through community outreach and doing good works?

Increasing a Company's Ability to Attract and Retain Employees

Companies seen as having a strong commitment to doing good often find it easier to recruit and retain employees, resulting in a reduction in turnover and associated recruitment and training costs.

Employers who encourage their personnel to volunteer for nonprofit organizations have an advantage when it comes to recruiting Generation Y. Nearly two-thirds of the respondents in the 2007 Volunteer IMPACT survey by Deloitte & Touche USA said they would prefer to work for companies that give them opportunities to contribute their talents to nonprofit organizations.[6]

"Several studies have shown that Gen Y employees want to make a positive difference in society, and, at the same time, nonprofits need help dealing with business and organizational issues in order to better deliver their social missions," said James H. Quigley, chief executive officer of Deloitte and Touche USA. "Companies that connect these two important realities, and encourage their people to contribute knowledge and experience to non-profits, will make a difference by giving back to the community—and at the same time build the skills and morale of their people."

The survey revealed that 80% of the respondents see themselves as volunteers, and 97 percent believe companies should offer their employees opportunities to volunteer.

Reducing Regulatory Oversight

Companies that demonstrably satisfy or go beyond regulatory compliance requirements are given more leeway by national and local government regulatory entities. In the U.S., for example, federal and state agencies overseeing environmental and workplace regulations have formal programs that recognize and reward companies that take proactive measures to reduce adverse environmental, health, and safety impacts. In many cases, such companies are subject to fewer inspections and paperwork, and may be given preference or "fast-track" treatment when applying for operating permits, zoning variances, or other forms of governmental permission. The U.S. federal sentencing guidelines allow penalties and fines against corporations to be reduced or even eliminated if a company can show it has demonstrated good corporate citizenship through its actions and that they have an effective ethics program in place.

Accessing Capital

Companies with strong performance in social responsibility have increased access to capital that might not otherwise have been available. Investors committed about $2.29 trillion to socially responsible strategies and communities in 2005, up from $2.16 trillion in 2003. Furthermore, shareholder resolutions on social and environmental issues increased more than 16 percent, from 299 proposals in 2003 to 348 in 2005.[7]

In its 2001 report on socially responsible investing in the United States, the Social Investment Forum reported that social investing rose to $2.34 trillion, despite an extended market downturn for most of the two-year period since the publication of the 1999 study. The primary driver for this growth was that socially concerned investors confined their portfolios to companies known for social responsibility practices. In 2001 this represented $2.03 trillion, up 36% from the 1999 $1.49 trillion. This amount accounts for nearly 12 percent of the $19.9 trillion in investment assets under professional management in the U.S.

Businesses should pay attention to this growing phenomenon if they want to grow their businesses and reap the benefits of corporate social responsibility.

Doing bad in the community has consequences.

We live in an era in which stories about corporate corruption make it to the front pages of newspapers on a frequent basis. Distrust of corporations rages throughout our communities, and it almost seems as if some executives spend more time in court than they do in their corner offices.

"Our shareholders have expectations" is a common refrain when corporate decision making results in huge price hikes for gasoline and other commodities but they are not talking about you and me. Most of a company's shareholders don't own enough stock to ever get rich or even gain much wealth.

Oil seeped into the tundra along the Alaska pipeline in 2006 from a spill of several hundred thousand gallons. According to a company spokesman, its inspectors were aware of corrosion in a pipeline months before it burst, but believed the threat to be low risk.[8] Well, that low risk resulted in a spill of nearly 300,000 gallons of oil. (Did the company fail to do preventative maintenance because of what it would do to profits?) When stories like these appear, is it any wonder that people lack trust in U.S. businesses? Every business suffers damage when any other business acts in an irresponsible and uncaring manner.

One final example of corporate greed: A headline in the March 15, 2006 *New York Times* article by David Cay Johnston reads, "Many Utilities Collect for Taxes They Never Pay." The article tells us that electric utilities collect billions of dollars from customers for corporate income taxes, which is legal. However, the utilities keep the money and the government never sees a penny of it. These same companies, according to the article, call this "smart business," and they justify it by saying that if they didn't use those tax dollars, they would have to raise rates.

Doing good in the community pays dividends.

There is good reason for politicians to make corporate values a political campaign issue. Polls show time and time again that Americans care about values.

In today's world, we divide politics into red states and blue states, primarily based on the perceived values held by the people living in those places. Car bumpers proudly display stickers proclaiming the values of their drivers. Tee shirts proclaim values, as do colored wrist bands and ribbons tied to trees. Businesses that fail to recognize the importance consumers place on what they believe and what they care about will not prosper. Their growth charts will look more like the Alps and less like the flight path of a plane taking off. We want others to know our values, and when they don't, we cannot understand why.

When you align your brand with a cause, you create an emotional bond with those consumers who also are aligned with that cause. And by effectively applying cause marketing to your outreach efforts, you increase sales and enhance brand loyalty, while building brand equity.

Here's what I mean: Yoplait raised more than $1.2 million for breast cancer awareness several years ago by having customers send in their Yoplait yogurt lids. For every lid mailed in, Yoplait donated 10 cents for breast cancer awareness. During that promotion, Yoplait reaped 12 million in sales. That ain't just yogurt; that's real revenue. What sales would they have reaped without the promotion? Who can say for certain? But what we can say is that Yoplait reaped millions of dollars in free marketing and advertising, and reached an audience they might not otherwise have reached. That is profitable in analysis.

Those numbers represent Yoplait's external efforts, but there usually is an internal return on investment as well. As mentioned earlier, today's recent graduates are looking for more than money in a job, and are willing to trade income to work for a company that is socially responsible and ethically minded. Employees of those companies are 25 percent more loyal than those working at companies who are not. This results in real cost savings:

Loyalty reduces turnover and raises earnings, because loyal employees as a rule are more productive.

Small businesses benefit as well as large companies. The owner of a small marketing firm in Connecticut supports professional women's organizations by giving of her time and offering small college scholarships. The positive public relations and word of mouth those cause-related efforts generate bring new clients. But this is not the primary reasons she gives back. She does it because it is the right thing to do. I know from experience that she would do these things whether or not she benefited financially, which makes her business authentically based in values. And many business people share that philosophy of genuinely wanting to give back.

Research and anecdotal evidence tells us time and time again that cause-related marketing, social responsibility, and ethics-driven business practices bring a good return on investment. And the more you share your commitment to the community and the planet using marketing, the greater your return on your good deeds.

Aligning with a Social Cause

Trying to get a fix on just how much businesses spend on social causes is a little tricky. However, it is clear that only a few of those companies who reach out charitably do so with strategies to enhance their brands, and that is a mistake. Doing good for others does not mean that you cannot do good for your business.

Only a fool ignores return on investment, even if that investment is directed at social causes. You have a business to run, and if you do it right, you will commit a percentage of your earnings to charitable and social causes. As your earnings grow, your giving should grow as well. Social causes reap the benefits of your giving, and your business reaps the benefits of increased earnings and growth. How can either of those things be bad?

This is a world where consumers have access to so much more information than they did even a decade ago. In the over-heated marketing world that we live in today, we are all bombarded daily with advertising, press releases, and other marketing communications that leave us in a daze. No wonder we have difficulty differentiating one company and its products and services from another.

Connecting your Brand to a cause and communicating that alignment appropriately endears your business to all stakeholders — from employees and customers to potential markets, customers, clients, and your shareholders. A 2001 Cone/Roper Corporate Citizenship Study found that 88 percent of employees are more engaged and loyal to their workplace when they become aware of the good works their company becomes involved in.

It is important to remember that cause-related marketing works better for some companies than for others. No amount of cause-related marketing would have helped Enron once the scandal broke or helped Exxon immediately after the Exxon Valdez oil spill.

But you can bring more attention to your Brand and make it more appealing and engaging to your employees and the public if it is associated with a cause embraced by the general public. Like everything else your company does, however, the cause you adopt must reflect your values. For example, if one of your values is to contribute positively to the environment, your company can get involved with a non-profit organization that devotes its energy to keeping the local waterways as clean as possible.

I once worked for a utility that adopted several acres of wetlands near its corporate headquarters. Each department would sign up for a weekend of clean-up with the local clean water association. It was fun! The local media usually ran a photo of us knee-deep in water or mud, and employees bonded around the cause. In addition to those clear benefits, our company became extremely aware of what we did with and to water, making us better stewards of our wetlands and waterways.

This cause aligned so perfectly with our values because we were one of a handful of businesses in a large metropolitan area that aligned itself with an environmental cause, so we stood out. Protecting the environment was also one of our core values. Only a few of the 2.5 million electric and gas users we served expected us to be concerned about the environment, so we received extra attention. People don't usually make a connection between an energy distributor and environmental protection, but we became better stewards of the land and water where our lines ran and our energy was produced, and embraced new, cleaner technologies. The environmental association we worked with, as well as others, recognized us for our efforts. In turn, we offered additional hours as volunteers and we wrote significant checks to help them with their work.

Some do, some don't.

Let's set something straight here: Not everyone embraces corporate social responsibility. In a 2005 debate held in London, the editor of *The Economist*, Mathew Bishop, had this to say: "Are companies actually socially irresponsible? I think the overwhelming message is that they are not. It has been the process of people seeking to make profit, and the expansion of an economic system where that pursuit of profit has been possible, that has made the world fantastically more wealthy than anyone thought possible, even 30 or 40 years ago."

Bishop supported his comments by saying that socially responsible businesses can lower shareholder returns, reduce focus by executives, and drive bad behavior into the shadows. He argued that using company money to support socially responsible causes was a misuse of shareholder money because the costs aren't directly related to the bottom line.

Business for Social Responsibility responded to Bishop's view by saying that corporate social responsibility and sound business practices go together, and social responsibility is good for businesses, shareholders, and society. The organization also noted that social responsibility is about long-term thinking and growth, whereas profits are short-term. Socially responsible companies it said, attract excellent employees who are more likely to be loyal customers. Thus, social responsibility builds respected brands.

➲ Practical and Tactical Advice ➲

The size of your business does not matter: Doing the right thing fits all sizes, but implementation must fit within your business structure. Consider such things as your size, your products and services, and your revenues. Here are a few tips to get your organization headed in the right direction:

- Give social responsibility a prominent position in your Mission Statement and make it one of your Core Values. It should also be built into your vision.

- Social responsibility cannot exist within a culture that marches in lockstep. Make innovation, calculated risk-taking, independence of thought, and good communication part of your culture.

- Make one group or one individual within your business responsible for the governance of your company.

- Make social responsibility part of your business plans, including your annual strategic plans.

- Make sure all responsibilities related to the company's social responsibility programs are written into individuals' job descriptions and evaluate their performance as it relates to those efforts.

- Create a system of recognition and rewards should be created to honor those who exceed your expectations in giving back to the community.

- When you prepare your Annual Report, make sure it contains a section detailing your engagement in socially responsible behavior, including your return on investment.

Benefiting from Corporate Social Responsibility

When corporate social responsibility becomes more than a popular catchphrase and businesses start to walk the talk, executives begin to realize that cause-related marketing reach a new target market, with the potential to bring in new customers. The benefits generally exceed expectations:

- Such companies make fewer environmental and social mistakes (which can cost some businesses millions, of dollars to repair).

- There is more customer loyalty.

- Corporate social responsibility separates you from the pack, which strengthens your Brand.

- Companies are able to hire, motivate, and retain a larger number of good employees when they are good corporate citizens.

Points to Ponder

- Corporate social responsibility initiatives can reduce operating costs dramatically.

- Customers often are drawn to brands and companies with a track record in corporate social responsibility.

- There's a growing market for the products and services of companies that are socially responsible.

- Like everything else your company does, the cause you take on must align with your values.

Chapter Eleven
You Can Change the World

The first thing I see when I go to turn on my computer each morning is a yellow Post-it Note that offers a quote from Mahatma Gandhi: "We must be the change we wish to see in the world." The quote underlines concepts that form the philosophical and business practices making up the Lead With Your Heart model presented in this book. I believe that businesses represent the best opportunity we have today to change the world. Your actions as a business leader touch and influence nearly every person on the globe, every second of every day of every year. What other institutions or enterprises hold such influence and power over people's lives?

Business has been about making as much money as possible for the few at the expense of the many. This has led to greed, malfeasance, and harm to the planet. Furthermore, it has prevented businesses from being as great as they otherwise could be.

When you lead with the heart, strive to increase happiness, and practice sound business practices, you and your enterprise will be profitable. Everyone wins, not just a few. Your business will produce positive changes in people's lives through its behavior, its products, and its services. Layoffs will be rare because they represent harm to the business in the long run. Employees and consumers will trust your Brand, and they will work hard to grow that Brand. The result will be a continuous flow of revenue into your business.

We owe it to our employees, our customers, our clients, our communities, our friends, our families, and ourselves to run ethical businesses in which all stakeholders win — not just those executives and shareholders who can afford great amounts of your stock. Winning needs to mean that all of us cross the finish line together as we make and sell great products and services and create great experiences for all. We are all in this together. There is no *us* versus *them*.

The Old Business Model vs. the Lead With Your Heart Model

GE's Jack Welch is still an icon and a powerful influence on MBA students. His idea of winning is reflected in GE's Mission Statement from 1981 through 1995. In his book *Winning*, he describes it this way: "To be the most competitive enterprise in the world by being No. 1 or No. 2 in every market — fixing, selling, or closing every underperforming business that couldn't get there." This is the opposite of the business model I am suggesting, which is people-centered. Jack Welch seems to believe that people are expendable and don't matter as much as making money. I disagree passionately!

The model followed by General Electric delivered extraordinary growth, increasing the market value of GE from just $12 billion in 1981 to about $280 billion in 1998. Net income went from approximately $2 billion in 1981 to nearly $9 billion in 1997. The company's revenue also jumped, from an already respectable $30 billion to $90 billion in 1997.

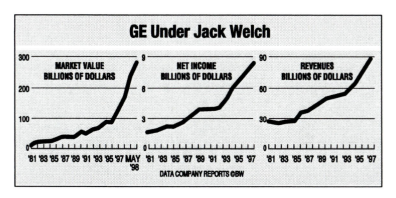

To a great extent, Welch reinvented GE, turning it into a global giant. Still, the focus remained on winning. We must also note that during Welch's leadership, there were several defense-contracting scandals and the Kidder, Peabody & Co. bond-trading scheme that generated bogus profits. GE bought the venerable 121-year old investment house Kidder, Peabody in 1986 for $600 million. GE's time on Wall Street was marked by financial scandals and waning profits at Kidder. I cannot prove that the mission statement Welch points to with pride led to the scandal (which was propagated by one employee, according to Welch), but Welch often uses sports metaphors to define "winning." Who among us does not believe that at least some athletes' competitiveness moves them to "do anything" to win, including cheating? If Welch gets credit for raising productivity and stockholder profits, then he also earns responsibility for the downsides, including the purchase of Kidder and the actions that led to the bond-trading scandal.

Still, Welch made this model work better than perhaps anyone before or since. And in at least one way, Welch models the business paradigm presented in this book, because he believes that there are no limits to human creativity.

"The idea flow from the human spirit is absolutely unlimited," Welch writes. "All you have to do is tap into that well. I don't like to use the word efficiency. It's creativity. It's a belief that every person counts."

But for Welch the goals are efficiencies, cost-cutting, stock value, and winning. At one of GE's legendary executive retreats, Welch said, "The market is rewarding you like Super Bowl winners or Olympic gold medallists. I know I have such athletes reporting to me. Can you put your team against my team? Are you proud of everyone who reports to you? If you aren't, you can't win. You can't win the game."

Welch's ability to create wealth for a few and grow GE comes out of the annals of John D. Rockefeller, who in the nineteenth century accumulated unparalleled wealth out of oil. Welch is the standard for the smart, innovative, and profit-focused business person. That is why I choose Welch as the primary example of what this kind of "winning" looks like in dollars earned. In this model, winners are few and losers are many. We can see the results of that business model in the following numbers:

From 1985 to 2005, the Consumer Price Index (CPI) increased 82 percent. Sounds good, except the reality of this index affects different people in different ways. During that same two-decade period, the average Fortune 500 company pay for CEOs, including salary and options exercised, grew from $1.2 million to $11.8 million (in 2005 dollars). This growth represents an 883 percent increase, which outpaced the Consumer Price Index by $9.6 million. At the same time, the average weekly pay for hourly workers grew from $305 to $551, an 81 percent increase that trails the CPI by $3. So while CEOs outpaced the CPI by $9.6 million, the average worker lost ground.

Focusing on the positive is always a good idea, but a business book urging a change in business practices must also provide examples of why dramatic change is so necessary. Picking on the airline industry may seem unfair, given their circumstances since September 11, 2001.

Do you know where your baggage is?

The Associated Press reported in March of 2006 that airlines temporarily lost 30,000,000 (that's right, million) pieces of luggage in 2005, of which 200,000 were never returned to their owners. Although this represents but 1 percent of the 3 billion bags that make their way through the world's airports, it is a 0.3 percent increase over 2004. It also represents lots of very unhappy, frustrated, and angry fliers who are more than willing to tell everyone they can about the airline that lost their bags.

Lost luggage in 2005 cost the airlines $2.5 billion. In an industry where businesses jump in and out of bankruptcy like they're in a game of hopscotch, you would think that after all these years they would be getting better at doing their jobs and creating happy customers. But try convincing fliers of that!

Not only do we have to worry about our baggage, but we also must deal with airport congestion, less-than-convenient terminal configurations, increased transfers and connections, and tighter security. None of these issues would make anyone look forward to flying. The airlines and the port authorities who host them must find better ways to manage their responsibilities. But most important, they must start to grasp the concept that business success is about creating a business that understands and meets the needs of its employees and its public.

The Lead With Your Heart Model

On the other end of the scale, consider the used-car giant CarMax. This company has a people-first attitude. It hires only people whose values are consistent with CarMax's values and who will fit well within the culture. Their hiring process includes an interview of some four hours. The price you see on the sticker is the price you get. Every sales person receives a flat commission on each car they sell, removing the impulse to sell someone a more expensive vehicle than they need. Buying a used car is not usually a great experience, but CarMax does everything it can to create one. They make buying a car easy, comfortable, and relatively safe from concerns about getting ripped-off.

The same can be said for the five-star Four Seasons hotel in Washington D.C., which is forever going the extra mile to ensure a great experience for every guest. (It once fulfilled a request to provide six Hummers for use by the children of a guest.)

These companies offer a stark contrast between the bottom-line way of running a business and the people-first way of running a business. At the end of the day, the differences tell us that a business model that is people-centered and values-based will, if managed properly, last longer and create better profits than the bottom-line model.

The difference between the business model I present here and the traditional one are obvious, as you can see from this chart:

Lead With Your Heart Business Model	**Bottom-Line** Business Model
• A culture based on values that are people-oriented. • Employees are self-actuated, innovative. and calculated risk-takers who believe and demonstrate that co-workers and customers are the most important factors in everything they say and do. • A passionate culture.	• A culture based on making money, with high employee turnover and fear of being fired if you fall in the bottom 10 percent (even if you are in the top 50 percent in your industry). • A culture ripe for scandal, rumor-mongering, and low productivity. • A culture that crushes innovation and creativity out of fear of failure. ("It's just a job.")
Great customer experiences	Uneven customer experiences
Products and services priced according to their value	Products and services priced according to competitors' prices
Potentially smaller revenues, with maximum profit margins	Potentially higher revenues, with uneven and almost certainly lower profit margins
Customer loyalty	High customer turnover
Employee loyalty	High employee turnover
Employees motivated by pride	Employees motivated by pay and benefits
Customers who take pride in their association with your brand	Customers who shop for price and who are not loyal to the brand

Wrapping Up

Far too many businesses—especially the largest ones in size and revenue—do a disservice to themselves, their shareholders, their employees, and their customers when they spend most of their working hours thinking about profit instead of using that time to create better experiences. And they don't even realize it.

Many executives who read this book believe that their primary responsibility is to their shareholders. They argue that they are responsible to Wall Street, not to Main Street. But if they feel really responsible to their shareholders, they would operate differently, because the majority of their shareholders are not the super rich (although the super rich might own a majority of the shares). They are average, hard-working people who will never become extremely wealthy. As one of those average shareholders, I believe most of us resent shareholders who pressure executives to focus on greed, short-term results, and profits instead of people.

Throughout this book, I have attempted to show that business owners *can* put people first and be values-based, long-term thinkers who believe that they are responsible first to their employees and then to their customers. And they can be socially responsible and *still* make lots of money!

The model does not promote social engineering. If you think it does, reread the book, especially those sections that talk about implementing strategies and tactics that boost sales and revenues. As I said at the beginning, I believe in capitalism, but I believe capitalism as it is practiced today hurts the majority of people and damages our planet. A business does not need to do either of these things in order to be profitable. Furthermore, I believe that the model presented here will grow both the top line and the bottom line with better margins than those businesses that are not people-centered.

I know this business model works because you and I have watched corporations such as Starbucks, Hewlett-Packard, Johnson & Johnson, 3M, and Wells Fargo implement many parts of it to become examples of America's most successful businesses. You know lots of small and medium-sized companies whose valuations are also rising dramatically because of the business philosophy expressed herein.

In order for a vast culture shift to take place, we must all strive to lead with our heart and to create happiness that touches all people. To do so, we must turn our companies into values-based businesses that meld best practices, innovation, and calculated risk taking. Then our businesses and people will prosper and *We will be the change we wish to see in the world.*

Thank you for taking the time to read this book. I hope that the philosophy resonates with you, and that you will prosper by growing a values-based business with a name that boasts a huge, oversized "B" in its public Brand image and Brand perception.

—Lewis Green

Notes

Chapter Two Notes

1. Datamonitor plc is a premium business information company specializing in industry analysis.

Chapter Four Notes

1. "2004 Customer Experience Management Study," by the Strativity Group, 139 Hillside Ave., Livingston, NJ 07039 (http://www.crmxchange.com/strativitygroup/).

2. Taken from Benchmark Portal, 3201 Airpark Dr. #104, Santa Maria, CA 93455 (http://www.benchmarkportal.com/newsite/index.tml).

3. See the Internet Retailer Survey from February, 2007 by Vertical Web Media, 300 S. Wacker Drive, Suite 602, Chicago, IL 60606 (http://www.internetretailer.com/article.asp?id=21292).

4. Passikoff is the founder and president of Brand Keys, publisher of the "Customer Loyalty Index" of leading companies in 26 product and service categories (since 1996).

Chapter Six Notes

1. Contact the Association of Management Consulting Firms at 380 Lexington Avenue, Suite 1700, New York, NY 10168 (212-551-7887, http://www.amcf.org).

Chapter Seven Notes

1. The Web site for Fred Wergeles & Associates is
   http://www.IntelStrategy.com

Chapter Eight Notes

1. See the 13th annual Sales Performance Optimization Study
   conducted by CSO Insights
   (http://www.csoinsights.com/index.htm).

Chapter Ten Notes

1. Business for Social Responsibility was founded in 1992 to
   help companies of all sizes and sectors achieve success in
   ways that demonstrate respect for ethical values, people,
   communities, and the environment. It is headquartered at
   111 Sutter Street, 12th Floor, San Francisco, California 94104.

2. The 2004 Cone Corporate Citizenship Study report presents
   the findings of a telephone survey conducted among a
   national probability sample of 1,033 adults comprising
   519 men and 514 women 18 years of age and older, who are
   living in private households in the continental United States.
   Interviewing for this CARAVAN Survey was completed by
   Opinion Research during the period October of 22–25, 2004.
   The margin of error is +/– three percentage points.

3. The March, 2007 study surveyed firms across a variety of
   industries to assess corporate sustainability practices and
   understand how sustainability is impacting businesses.
   Corporate sustainability is defined as "the promotion of
   economic development (e.g., profits and job creation),
   environmental stewardship (e.g., energy conservation
   and pollution reduction), and social well-being (labor
   standards and community impact)."

4. The 2007 Cone Consumer Environmental Survey presents the findings of an online survey conducted March 29, 2007 by Opinion Research Corporation of 1,066 adults (499 men and 567 women, 18 years of age and older). The margin of error associated with a sample size of 1,000 is +/- 3%.

5. Connecting People to What Matters" is the latest report in the Deloitte Research Talent Management series: "It's 2008: Do You Know Where Your Talent Is?" More information on the series and a copy of the report is available by contacting Britton Josey at 404-220-1334 or bjosey@deloitte.com, or by linking to www.deloitte.com/us/connect.

6. Opinion Research Corporation (ORC) conducted a national online survey of 1,000 adults between the ages of 18 and 26. ORC maintains a Web-based data-collection operation that is responsible for programming and the output of data collected via the Web. The sample for the study came from the Research Now online panel. There was a 3.2 percent margin of error for questions asked of all respondents, and a 3.6 percent margin of error for questions asked of only those who are employed. (However, this does not take other sources of error into account. This online survey is not based on a probability sample, and therefore no theoretical sampling error can be calculated.) Data collection commenced on February 21 and concluded on February 27.

7. 2005 Report on Socially Responsible Investing Trends in the United States, available from the Social Investment Forum Industry Research Program (1612 K Street NW, Suite 650, Washington, D.C. 20006).

8. See "Company Knew about Corrosion in Alaska Pipeline Before Spill," in *The Mining Journal,* (Alaska's Upper Peninsula) for March 15, 2006.

Resources

Boston College Center for Corporate Citizenship. *2007 Report on Business Leadership* (February, 2007).

Collins, Jim. 2001. *Good to Great.* New York: HarperCollins.

Collins, Jim and Jerry I. Porras. 1994. *Built to Last.* New York: HarperBusiness.

Cone, Carol L., Mark A. Feldman, and Alison T. DaSilva. 2003. Align Your Brand With a Social Cause. *Harvard Business School Working Knowledge* (July 14, 2003).

Covey, Steven R. 2006. *The 8th Habit: From Effectiveness to Greatness.* New York: Free Press.

EMarketer. 2007. Half of Customer E-Mail Goes Unanswered (April, 2007).

Gaffney, John. Superbrands, Advocacy, Obsession: The Five Elements of Customer Engagement That Take Customer Relationships Beyond Loyalty, published in *1to1 Magazine* (October, 2005).

Gladwell, Malcolm. 2000. *The Tipping Point.* Little, Brown.

Global Insight. 2005 study "U.S. Direct Marketing Today: Economic Impact 2005."

Haar, Dan. 2006. "Sikorsky Strike: Universal Struggle," published in *The Hartford Courant* (March 12, 2006).

Jaworski, Bernard J. and Jeffrey F. Rayport. 2005. *Best Face Forward: Why Companies Must Improve Their Service Interfaces with Customers.* Harvard Business School Press.

Kalra, Ritu. 2005. "No Thanks to Corporate World, Business Careers Lose Allure for More Young Women," published in *The Hartford Courant* (November 4, 2005).

Leahy, Ted. 2003. Strategic Planning Meets Business Performance. *Business Finance* (February, 2003).

Manifesto Challenge: Encouraging Enterprise. (Royal Society for the Encouragement of Arts; Manufactures and Commerce; and Economist Debate "Companies That Put Time and Money into Corporate Social Responsibility are Digging Their Own Grave.") April, 2005. RSA.

Marakon Consulting. 2005. Closing the Strategy-to-Performance Gap, in *Harvard Business Review* (July/August, 2005).

Passikoff, Robert. 2005. The Five Keys to Branding Success in 2006, in *Chief Marketer*.

Peppers, Don and Martha Rogers. 2005. The Essence of Strategy, in *Return on Customer Monthly* (July 28, 2005).

Peppers, Don and Martha Rogers. 2005. Customer Acquisition: How Can Executives Measure New Customer Value? in *Return on Customer Monthly* (June 23, 2005).

Reichheld, Fred. 2006. *The Ultimate Question: Driving Profits and True Growth.* Harvard Business School Press.

Shaw, Stephen. 2005. All That Should Ever Matter Is What Really Matters to Customers, in *Marketing* (December, 2005)

Social Investment Forum Industry Research Program. 2005. *Report on Socially Responsible Investing Trends in the U.S. for 2005.* (1612 K Street N.W., Suite 650; Washington, D.C. 20006).

Trunk, Penelope. 2007. *Brazen Careerist: The New Rules of Success.* New York: Warner Business Books.

Welch, Jack with Suzy Welch. 2005. *Winning.* New York: HarperBusiness.

Williams, Simon. 2004. The Ten New Rules of Branding, in *Chief Marketer.*

Wulfhorst, Ellen. 2006. Americans Work More, Seem to Accomplish Less. *Reuters* (February 23, 2006).